Answers
for
Airline Passengers

Jan C. Ramos

Home Publishing Company

P.O. Box 130

Rocklin, CA 95677

ISBN: 0-9672645-0-2

Edited by Cynthia Casanova

Cover Design and Graphic Production by
Michelle Roth Design
Sacramento, California

Printed by Paul Baker Printing, Inc.
Roseville, California

Acknowledgements

First I'd like to thank my parents, Dr. Carol D. Ramos, who holds a Ph.D. in Linguistics, and Arthur C. Ramos, Professor of Physics and Physical Science, for sharing their vast knowledge in their respective fields, as well as the use of the family airplane, N1009M.

I'd also like to thank my sister, Vicki L. Ramos, who is also an Airline Pilot, for inspiring me to fly. Without her encouragement to fly, I'm sure I would have continued in the medical field.

I'm indebted to Vicki Husted of Administrative Alternatives, for all her skills on the computer in helping with this book.

And finally, thanks to all the wonderful people in this world who have given me input for this book, and whom I consider to be my friends.

ANSWERS FOR AIRLINE PASSENGERS

CONTENTS

PREFACE

Before the first word was written in this little book, I knew that I wanted to write down my thoughts for others. As time passed, my enthusiasm built day by day as I did my research.

Thanks to you, the many airline passengers who have flown with me, and to those who hope to take their first trip by airplane, I did personal research with hundreds of people over a period of time.

I was amazed how a little information regarding flying would capture their interest and generate questions that they wanted answers to, so that they could feel more at ease on their trips.

They provided the questions, and I was determined to provide them answers—truthfully, and in language that even a young person could appreciate. I met with all of these wonderfully interesting people in hotels, airports, restaurants, and—even on the streets—to answer any question about flying.

After a few months of mingling with those who wish to travel, I began to notice that questions kept repeating themselves. So, I wrote down the questions on paper. And since I had committed the questions to paper, I decided that I really should write down the answers, too . . . thus, the inception of my book.

I hope that passengers and passengers-to-be will continue to ask questions about the crew, the plane, and the flight, so that they may enjoy and appreciate this remarkable way of travel that has become essential in our lifetime.

Happy Landings,

CHAPTER 1. INTRODUCTION

This little book contains an explosion of material just waiting for your attention.

This writer will accompany you on your trip from the time you reach the airport until you arrive at your destination.

I have grouped the questions you may have into chapter headings, and have made the answers as full as they need to be for your understanding and enjoyment of the trip.

Even when you are stressed because of an airline decision, or feeling like you have no control, having some understanding of the situation helps—along with patience.

I suggest that you read this book the first time as an introduction to new material, and a second time for enjoyment and discussion.

And please . . . the next time you decide to fly . . . share your new knowledge with those around you! You'll be surprised just how interested they will be!!!

CHAPTER 2. SCHEDULING

This chapter concerns itself with arrival and departure delays, and the over-booking of flights.

If an airline has 1,000 flights a day, how many schedulers are there and how do they go about their work? (Before computers, imagine doing it by hand.) Some passengers blame the ticket agents for changes in the schedules. Perhaps, if they knew all the factors that have caused the delay, they would keep their "cool."

Delays

Calling ahead to check your flight will allow you time to prepare for possible changes, rather than being surprised.

To check your flight status, just call the telephone number of the airline, give them your name, flight number, date of travel, confirmation number, and ask your ticket agent if your space is secure for a seat on the aircraft. If you are traveling on "seats available", or standby, the agent will try to accommodate you by looking at the seating availability of other flights. Be sure to look at your ticket carefully so you don't confuse the check-in time with your departure time. This happens often!

Delays usually increase as the day progresses, because of changes in weather and from mechanical difficulties, often due to constant use of the planes. This can result in cancellations and missed flights. You're better off to schedule an early morning flight, because it reduces the chances of delays, cancellations, and over-booking.

Arriving at your airport too late can cause you to miss your flight and also the connecting flight. You may also find that the next flight out is "over-booked" as well.

If at all possible, call your airline if something beyond your control has caused you to be late for your flight, so that they may start solving your problem immediately by re-booking you on a later flight.

Why Is My Aircraft Late?

Delays that are announced when you are at the gate can occur for several reasons:

1. Additional fuel needs to be added at the last minute because the destination airport's weather is deteriorating at the time of scheduled arrival.

2. Due to increasing temperature, the aircraft's take-off weight is limited and making it necessary to unload some cargo.

3. Due to snow or ice accumulating on the wings, the aircraft gets de-iced at the gate or prior to departure.

4. A mechanical problem occurs prior to push-back.

5. Changing of the Flight Crew may cause a delay. Even though this may be your first flight of the day, the Pilots may be at the end of their day. Federal Aviation Administration (FAA) rules state that Pilots can't fly more than 8 scheduled hours in a day, 30 hours in 7 consecutive days, or 100 flight hours in a calendar month. The final restriction is 1,000 flight hours in a calendar year. These restrictions pertain to domestic flights only. These are flight hours, not on-duty hours (i.e., pre-flight, etc.). Some airlines may restrict flight and duty hours even further.

6. Crew rest requirements also affect the departure schedule. If your Flight Crew is scheduled for a minimum crew rest at their final destination and their arrival time is delayed, then the crew rest will start at the time they land at the final destination. The new departure time from that city will be after the minimum rest period, regardless of the original scheduled departure time. This occurs if the in-bound Flight Crew takes the first out-bound flight in the morning. (This is an FAA rule.) So your morning departure can be delayed if the same crew is being utilized.

7. An aircraft swap may be required due to a mechanical delay, or the airlines may need to utilize a larger aircraft to accommodate the passengers.

8. Your arriving airplane may have previously encountered a departure delay at it's departing airport.

9. The arrival aircraft is in holding due to congestion at the airport, or due to weather conditions.

10. Gate holds may occur when your destination airport is saturated with aircraft on the ground, on an approach, and already holding. The destination airport will send out a message to delay further incoming aircraft to prevent further congestion.

11. Even special requests from dignitaries can cause a ground stop, as well as gate holds.

Some of these topics are covered in greater detail in the chapters that follow.

Over-Booking Flights

It is the business of the airline to provide the size of plane to accommodate the number of reservations for the particular time slot and destination. Over the years, airline schedulers have found that some people don't show up for their reserved seats, resulting in a large loss of revenue.

It is a practice for an airline to "over-book", that is, reserve more seats than the seating capacity of the plane. If you find that you have purchased a ticket and cannot be seated on your plane, then it is the responsibility of the airline to find you a seat on another flight or offer other accommodations, free of charge. The airline needs satisfied customers!

Once boarding of the aircraft has begun, you should board as early as possible. If you are wondering why you should board when the plane will not lift off for another fifteen minutes, there are several reasons why:

1. There is the chance of duplicate seat assignments, which take time to be corrected.

2. You may discover that there is no remaining space in the overhead compartment and you may have to gate check your bag, in which case the airline will have to transfer it to the baggage compartment of the aircraft.

3. A final passenger count must be made to determine the weight and balance of the plane. If fewer passengers show up, the airline can put on additional cargo or remove it, if the aircraft is sold out. This cannot be determined until you're seated.

4. If you wait until the last minute, any or all of these can happen to you, causing a delay. Then the other 100 or so passengers will be wondering why you didn't board the plane with the rest of them.

Travel Agency Booking

If you decide to book your flight through a travel agency, there are a few things that you should know. The airlines allow approximately 70% (it varies with each airline) of the aircraft's confirmed seats to be released and assigned to passengers regardless of where they get their ticket. The remaining approximately 30% of the aircraft seat assignments will be available on the day of departure.

If you were unable to receive an advance seating assignment, it is highly recommended that on the day of departure you arrive at least 1-2 hours or more prior to your scheduled departure. The remaining day-of-departure seat assignments are released between 2-4 hours prior to departure, depending on the airline. So if you're late checking in to receive a seat, you may end up with only your ticket, and not a seat. Call the airline for specifics.

Airlines will not release emergency row seats until the day of departure because the airlines want to make sure that the person receiving the exit row seat is:

1. Of age (over 15 years old);

2. Physically able to assist with the exit row procedures;

3. Willing to perform the exit row procedures;

4. Able to read written English and understand spoken English.

If you're traveling on an airline that doesn't offer seat assignments, and you want to sit next to the person you're traveling with, it's a good idea to be at the check-in counter at least one hour prior to departure so you can get low-numbered boarding passes. The first 80 or so passengers boarding will have their choice of seats, usually leaving center seats only.

Another problem that can cause over-booking is a passenger who shops around with travel agencies for airline prices and books a reservation on the same flight several times with the different agencies. Please cancel or advise the travel agency to cancel previous reservations and seat assignments, or only make a reservation/ seat assignment with the agency you are pleased with.

This chapter was written to help ease some of the tensions that may develop before checking in. Among the problems and solutions that are discussed are passengers with special needs, unaccompanied minors, pets, stand-bys and more. An important reminder: as you move through the terminal, please read all the signs. It will reduce your stress and expedite you to your final destination.

Passengers with Tickets and Luggage

If you decide to check your bags with the sky cap (outside) you will need to have an E-Ticket, airline ticket, or have a reservation in the airline computer system for that flight plus an I.D. card. It's great for convenience, but keep in mind that checking your bags does not mean that you've checked in for the flight. You still need to check-in at the gate or at the airline counter for your boarding ticket. If you don't, you may find yourself standing in lines unnecessarily: First when your row is called, and next when you must go to the gate counter to check-in, then in the boarding line again. It is also in your best interest to remove all <u>old</u> previous destination tags, as the final destination could be confused by the baggage handlers.

Carry-on luggage is normally restricted to two bags, and is also restricted to certain dimensions. It is highly recommended to check with the airline you're traveling on for their specific dimensions, as they can vary between airlines. This will be less worry for you.

If you have alcohol in your carry-on luggage, it's best that it remains there because it can be an offense of Federal Aviation Regulation 121.575 to consume it while you are on the aircraft. Also, passengers may be denied boarding if they appear to be intoxicated or are otherwise acting erratically.

If you'd like to go "bagless", contact your local air freight airline and send your bags a day or so ahead of your flight. The cargo airlines can have your luggage delivered to your destination (hotel, ski resorts, or Grandma's house) insured and guaranteed with a tracking number. All you'll need to do then is contact the destination to confirm the luggage has arrived. Now you can truly sit back, relax, and enjoy the flight.

I've noticed some passengers get to the airport several hours early and want to check their bags on the next available flight to their destination, even though the flight may be sold out. The reason the airlines will not accept the luggage in those circumstances is because of increased security requirements. Because of previous terrorist problems, the airlines must match the luggage with the passenger. Also, you would run a higher risk of a lost bag or someone else picking up your luggage instead of theirs.

The risk of having your luggage stolen increases around holidays. Unfortunately, there are a few individuals just waiting for the opportunity to steal your fine gifts.

Unaccompanied Minors

Most airlines define unaccompanied minors (UMs) as children between the ages of five and twelve who are unaccompanied by an adult.

Sometimes the routing of the aircraft determines what rules apply; for instance, flying internationally requires an earlier check-in time than domestic routes, and the children must have a letter from the parents, allowing them to fly internationally.

Usually, most airlines charge about $30.00 domestic and $50.00 international each way for a minor needing assistance.

1. Early Check-In: Call the airline to get the information you'll need and to arrange a check-in time (about 1 ½ hours ahead of scheduled departure time). On the UM form, be sure to fill in the name, address, and phone number of the responsible person who will be dropping off and picking up the child. Also, be sure to advise the responsible person that they must have a photo identification readily available. When dropping a child off for a flight, the responsible person should remain at the departure gate until the aircraft actually departs.

2. Instruction by Flight Attendant: Among the Flight Attendant's duties are:

a) To make sure that identification papers are completed by the sending adult with the name, address, and phone number of the receiving adult.

b) To board the child early enough to teach the needed safety requirements and the demonstration of the minor's mastering these tasks. Tasks include fastening the seatbelts correctly, using the oxygen mask, should it deploy, understanding seat cushion flotation, finding the location of exits, and locating the call button, to mention a few. The Flight Attendant will then have the minor demonstrate that they understand the correct way of doing the above procedures. If there is doubt that the child understands, the Flight Attendant will repeat the process until the child can do it correctly. ***Don't be late***.

c) The airlines prefer to board the children first to give them the one-on-one attention and the additional time that they may need in getting comfortable. Also the children normally get off last, so that they can be in sight of the Flight Attendant at all times. Some airlines will not let the child board the last flight of the day, because of the possibility of cancellations or delay on the next segment of their flight.

d) If the child is, or will be, taking medicine, the Flight Attendant will need to know all the information concerning the medication and the dosage required. Most airlines require a written letter stating what medications are to be taken, when to administer it, and how. The airlines have had children board with their medication, but without instructions, and having no idea of the proper dosage. Please don't let this happen to your child.

e) The child needs to tell the Flight Attendant if the person next to them makes them uncomfortable, so the Flight Attendant will move the child to another seat.

f) Because the Flight Attendants have other passengers to attend to, as well as your child, it is very important that you provide your child with their own entertainment. You know how energetic children can be; just imagine having your child seated for an hour or two, and then you will know what will hold their attention span and will also keep them seated (i.e., toys, books, crossword puzzles, etc.).

Passengers Who Show Up Late or Are Flying Stand-By

Passengers who show up late or those on stand-by tickets, must respect the rules of the airline. Most of the time there will be a seat available. If you have called the airline to check on your status, you will be informed if it appears that there will be enough seats available or if the plane is full. Depending on the airline, they may release your seat 10-20 minutes prior to departure for domestic flights or 60-90 minutes for international flights if you have not checked in. These seats will then be given away to stand-by passengers. This usually is stated on or inside the ticket jacket. It doesn't matter if you bought your ticket full-fare or a month ago, the 10-20 minute final call applies. Also, if the flight is over-sold, those passengers who checked in last are usually the ones who get bumped first. It is also highly recommended if you are traveling on a pass or stand-by, to try and fly out early in the day, as this will give you more opportunities to arrive at your final desti-nation in the <u>same</u> day.

Special Needs: Wheelchairs, Aisle Chairs, Meet & Assist Services, Seatbelt Extensions, Special Meals, Chapels, Military Assistance, Aisle Seats, Seat Assignments

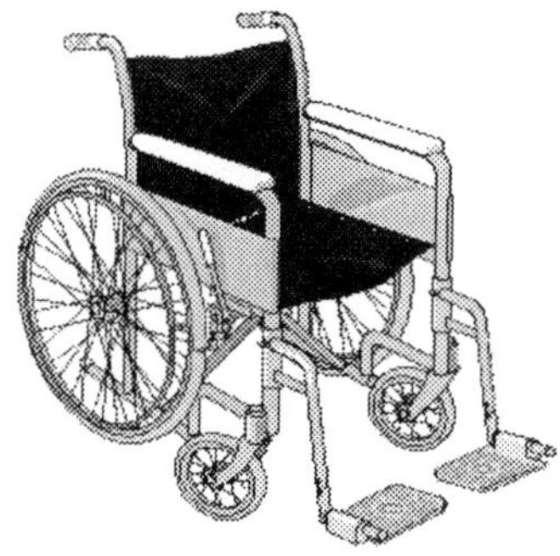

If you know that you need, or will need a wheelchair, it is best at the time of your reservation to mention your need, then mention your needs again at the gate check-in, and also to the Flight Attendant. If you forget, don't worry, just tell the Flight Attendant as you board the plane; and they will tell the Pilots. Before the Pilots start their descent into the airport (usually about 30 minutes out), they will call to find out information about the gate location, the next destination for the aircraft, and where close connections are departing from. Also, at that time they will request wheelchairs, aisle chairs, and Meet & Assist services. For your convenience there are two sizes of wheel-chairs and aisle chairs at most airports.

Meet & Assist is a service provided for those passengers who may speak another language including sign language, or are dis-oriented, blind, handicapped, or elderly, requiring personal assis-tance. In some cases a personal escort may be needed.

If you require any of the above, ask for an aisle seat when you make your flight reservation; otherwise you may get a medically dif-ficult-to-manage seat (i.e., a window seat). Also, on a long flight, you may wish to have a seat close to a restroom, for your convenience.

Be sure to inform the Flight Attendant of other medical prob-lems, such as diabetes, seizure disorders, heart problems, and asthma. If you're diabetic, it's a great idea to bring any special foods onto the aircraft. Most domestic flights' snacks are limited to nuts, pretzels, and raisins. Even these snacks can be delayed in reaching you because of departure delays or turbulence. For this same reason, it's wise to take any needed medications and water prior to boarding the aircraft. Bring all of your medicines and hand-held medical equipment on board with you; otherwise you will not have access to it. If you put them in luggage that was checked, they will be in the baggage compartment, unavailable if you need them. Also keep in mind most airlines are not equipped to refrigerate your medications. The best they can do is offer you ice, and the amount can be limited. There are no refrigerators on board most aircraft, especially domestic aircraft.

Seatbelt extensions are available on all flights, simply by requesting them from the Flight Attendants.

If you require a special diet, most airlines offer a wide variety of special meals. Some more common ones are low calorie, kosher, low cholesterol, low sodium, vegetarian, baby and child meals, and diabetic meals. They are available at no extra cost to you. Although these are available, it is recommended that you call the airline 24 hours in advance of your scheduled flight to request them, even if you made this request at the time your reservation was made. That will help to ensure that you receive your special meal. To be absolutely sure, carry your own food from home.

Almost all of the large airports offer USO or military assistance for active, retired, or reserve military. Some of the assistance can include, but is not limited to lounges for reading, watching television, light entertainment, showering, and of course, resting and complimentary food.

Chapels and/or Chaplains can also be located at most major airports. Just check with the information desk for their location.

Pets

Most airlines charge $50.00 for domestic and $90.00 for international flights, though exact costs depend on the size and weight of the animal. Airlines require that you have shot records for your pet that are current within 30 days of your flight. Check with your airline.

While you are preparing your pets for a flight, keep in mind that if you have to sedate them, you'll want to make sure your departing flight is on time. You wouldn't want the medication to wear off too early or be unable to give additional sedation. If you are sending your pet on a connecting flight, it's a good idea, before you board your pet, to see where the connecting flight is coming in from and to check if it is delayed greatly. If it is delayed, you may want to make arrangements for another flight. If you are continuing on with your pet and your connecting flight is delayed, you may, depending on the airline, check your pet to see if it needs any medication, food, or water. Another helpful thing to do is to freeze water in the animal's drink container for the flight, because it is very easy to spill in the loading process. Most airlines offer plastic water and food dishes. You may pick up the necessary paperwork (or request it be mailed to you) and dishes in advance of your flight, to make it less stressful on both of you.

Federal rules prohibit airlines from leaving your pets in cargo holds for greater than 45 minutes in temperatures exceeding 85°F. or of 45°F. or less, so try not to worry.

Service Animals:

Seeing-Eye, Hearing, and Search Dogs are not restricted in the cabin, but must be accompanied by an impaired person or handler. Service dogs must be harnessed and seated on the floor in front of the impaired person or handler. They cannot be seated in the emergency row. Most airlines will charge a fee for the service animal's flight.

Companionship Dogs:

These are dogs which are used for the comfort of an impaired person (e.g., someone with cerebral palsy, wheelchair-bound, or someone who is unable to use their arms, etc.). These dogs can open doors, pick up dropped items, retrieve newspapers and turn on/off lights to name a few of their tasks. Companionship dogs are allowed on the aircraft as long as they are harnessed, and the impaired person or trainer accompanies them. They will also sit on the floor in front of the impaired person or trainer, and must not be in an exit row seat.

On some airlines, celebrity pets (i.e., Lassie, Eddie, the dog on Frasier, RCA Dogs, etc.) are permitted on the aircraft and assigned a seat just as though they were normal passengers. However, the animal has to be the celebrity, not its owner, unless they both happen to be celebrities.

All of the above-mentioned pets are subject to quarantine at the destination, either domestic or abroad, depending on the state laws. It's a good idea to check out the laws of the state prior to your trip; airlines are aware of them. The airlines normally will put your pet on board last, and pets will be the first ones off if transported in the cargo bay, for the pet's comfort.

Cellular Phones

Cellular phones may be used on the aircraft only while it is at the gate and the doors are open. It is an offense of Federal Aviation Regulation 91.21, which regulates portable electronic devices, to use a cellular phone on the aircraft after the aircraft doors are closed.

Some airlines restrict the use of cellular phones even further. Please check the briefing card, air carrier magazine, or ask the Flight Attendant about the restrictions.

Have you wondered why you can't use your own cellular phone, but you can use the aircraft's in-flight phone? The in-flight phone system is shrouded, which prevents radio waves from interfering with the navigational equipment, whereas the cellular phones' radio waves are not shrouded.

Smoking

Smoking is prohibited on all domestic flights and on many international flights. If passengers attempt to smoke on an aircraft while the No Smoking sign is illuminated, they can be fined up to $3,300 for violating Federal Aviation Regulation 121.571. This federal law also prohibits tampering with, disabling, or destroying any smoke detector in an airplane lavatory; smoking in lavatories; and, when applicable, smoking in passenger compartments.

In addition to the regular smoke detectors, several types of aircraft are equipped with sensors that activate a caution light in the Flight Deck when there is any smoke in the lavatories. If you must smoke, please do so before boarding the aircraft.

In-Flight Library

All airline magazines have so much information to offer to you, other than advertisements. And guess what, they're FREE!! You can take the magazine off the airplane and share it with a friend who may be traveling soon. Most airlines update their magazines once a month. Some great information in the magazine includes: upcoming events, stories, coupons/discounts on car rental, restaurants and hotels, crossword puzzles, airline directories, airport terminal layouts, airline route maps, in-flight movie listings, audio entertainment listings, and the refreshment list. By reviewing the refreshment list, you will know what that particular airline offers, as catering varies from airline to airline.

And for those who love to shop, wait no longer; the Sky Mall magazine located in the seatback of most aircraft is available so that you may enjoy catalog shopping in the air or on the ground. This magazine consists of a wide variety of advertisements for food, clothes, tools, and furniture just to mention a few. This magazine also consists of portions of several well known catalogs, and is free for you to take home.

Available for your reading pleasure is an in-flight library. Every airline subscribes to different magazines, so depending on the airline, you may see magazines such as : Business Week, P.C. World, Worth, Forbes, Working Woman, Success, Car & Driver, Tennis, Golf, Boating World, and National Geographic, to list a few that are available to you, just for the asking. The list may also vary depending upon the length of the flight. Keep in mind, these do remain on the airplane, unless the Flight Attendant says otherwise.

Medical Kits on Board

Medical kits and first aid kits are installed on all commercial aircraft. The medical kit(s), depending on the size of the aircraft, is located in the Flight Deck and can be used only by licensed medical personnel. The items in the medical kit usually include, but are not limited to, a blood pressure cuff, stethoscope, tourniquets, surgical gloves, syringes, needles and swabs, plus certain vital medications, including nitroglycerin tablets.

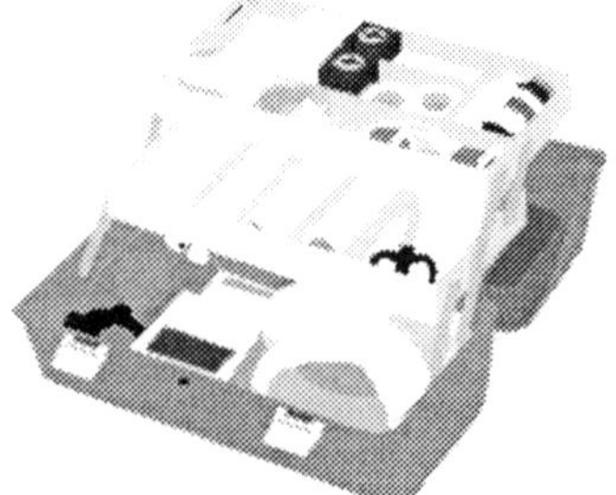

The first aid kits which are located in the cabin usually contain bandages, adhesive tape, scissors, splints, burn ointments, antiseptic swabs, ammonia inhalants, CPR mask, and certain medicines, such as aspirin, Motrin and Tylenol.

Both of these types of kits are inspected and restocked if anything was used during that crew's flight, prior to every originating departure, or if there is a crew change.

Portable oxygen is always available for you in a medical emergency.

Medical Personnel and Pilots on Board; Pilots Able to Contact Emergency Room Doctors in Minutes

Did you know that on an average flight, you will have at least three medical personnel and two Pilots amongst the passengers on board? They may or may not work for that particular airline, and may be going to a convention, meeting, work, or even on vacation, just as you might be.

Did you know that the Pilots at any altitude can contact an Emergency Room Doctor usually within 2 minutes? All airlines are equipped to perform a phone patch between an Emergency Room Doctor and the Pilots. The Pilots, Flight Attendants, and Emergency Room Doctor work together to determine whether to divert the flight or continue on. If there is a Medical Doctor on board (and chances are good there may be), they also can aid in making the determination.

The airlines really do care for you and your well-being while you are in their care. The Flight Deck and Cabin Crew do more than just give Public Address announcements.

CHAPTER 4. PRE-FLIGHT

In pre-flight, the airplane must be made ready; the crew must review their charts, instruments, destination, and of course, the weather. While the Flight Attendants prepare the cabin, passengers have the task of making themselves ready, too. This chapter discusses the awesome job of getting everything done, almost simultaneously so that we can do what we have all been waiting to do—take off!

Did you know, before the first flight takes place, and after every Flight Crew change, a Pilot will perform a thorough inspection of the exterior and interior of the aircraft?

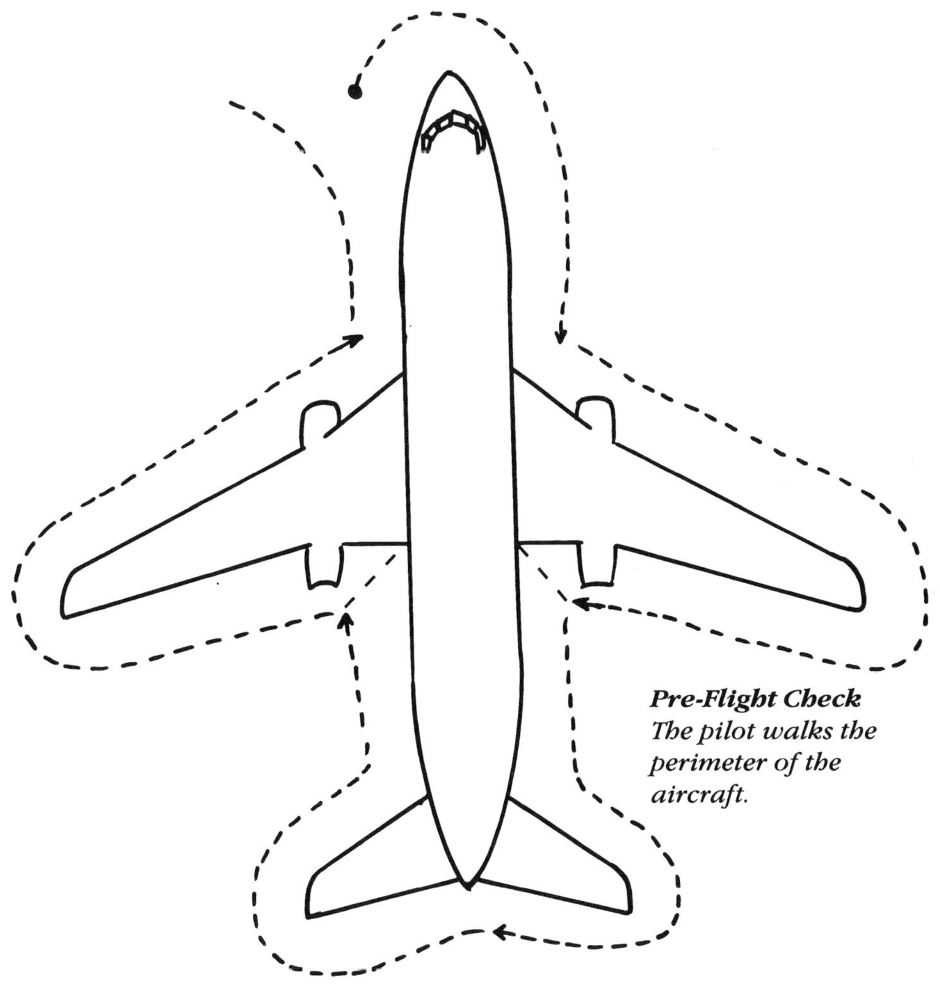

Pre-Flight Check
The pilot walks the perimeter of the aircraft.

The Pilot is looking at the aircraft in a systematic way, starting at the nose of the aircraft continuing around the entire plane, to check for anything that is loose, any leaks, evidence of bird strikes, or anything unusual. They are also looking at the landing gear and tires for normal wear. This inspection is to insure the aircraft is in an excellent airworthy condition that meets the airline requirements and FAA requirements. Meanwhile, the Flight Attendants are checking the inside of the aircraft cabin's safety equipment and all other essentials for the flight. If the aircraft falls short of these strict requirements, the aircraft will receive maintenance, repair, or a replacement of the problem item. If this can't be done in a timely matter, another aircraft may be substituted.

The word "delay" can trigger the worst fears or aggravations when you're ready to fly. You've worried all night and fought traffic to get to your flight, just to learn that all you can do is hurry up and sit down. This chapter concerns itself with the major causes of delays. After discussion of the reasons for delays, I hope the reader will appreciate why there are delays and list them under the heading of "Safety Precautions."

Flying by plane is a relatively new concept in transporting the masses. Not too many decades ago, it was the affluent who paid the price for the airline tickets. There were no "cheap" fares. Of course, these ticket holders expected the best of everything—in personal service, the flight, the luggage handled for them, and even larger seats.

The streamlined method of transportation enjoyed this luxury image for many years. But as time passed, schedules and destination became more important.

During the mid-1950's, airplanes were built larger, engines were stronger, more seats were installed (and they were smaller), thus increasing the aircraft's carrying capacity. Instead of climbing up an outside ladder to the plane, "jetways" were built to transport passengers from the airport to the outside door of a waiting plane. Fewer crew members were needed and distances between fill-ups increased.

After these changes were made, the airlines could offer more people transportation at much lower prices.

In addition to the complexity of increased numbers of passengers being transported, there are other possible causes for delays.

Weather

To go or not to go—that is the question.

When deciding whether to drive your car, have you ever said, "I think I'll wait until it has quit raining or snowing or until the wind dies down"? Maybe you have thought it was too hot or too cold to drive.

Airline Pilots make these same decisions every day. Before take-off and landing of your flight, they study the weather reports and the weather radar all along the distance to your destination. They make decisions about windshear, icing, and lightning.

For your peace of mind, let's study some of the weather phenomena. Weather can be defined as the current condition of the atmosphere; that is, cold, hot, rainy, sunny, icy, snowy, etc.; as opposed to the word "climate", which describes the above conditions most likely to happen over a long period of time.

The airlines and those who represent them are confident that most of the passengers have experienced, at one time or another, most of the conditions of weather, and sometimes in combination—that is—you may have experienced a hot, windy, rainy morning with an abundance of thunder and lightning. Do you remember the decisions that you made before driving that day? You probably made the decision to stay at home until the storm had passed, even though you risked being late for a very important appointment.

Pilots make those same decisions not to "take-off" nor "land" under these weather conditions. So your flight may be late, in the name of safety. As a passenger, how do you feel about the delay? Are you angry or thankful?

Weather is a very significant factor in an aircraft's ability to take-off and to land safely. Once we reach the cruising altitude, we are above the weather conditions below, until we approach our destination.

Two other weather conditions that affect aircraft, icing and windshear, will be explored next.

Windshear

Windshear is a change in wind direction and velocity within a short distance. Let's discuss situations involving windshears aloft.

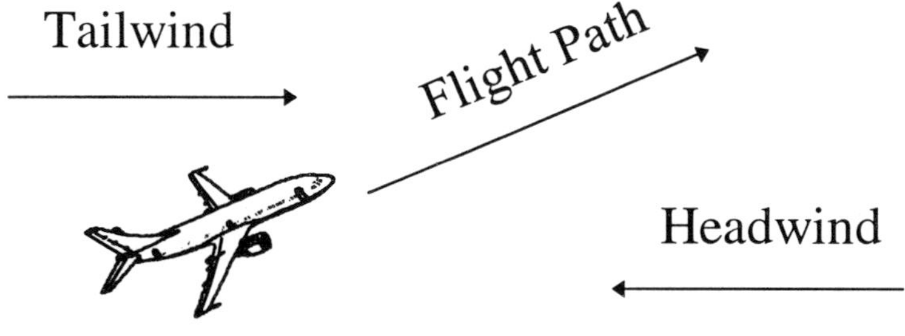

When an aircraft flies against the wind, it is referred to as a headwind, and when the aircraft is flying with the wind, it is referred to as a tailwind.

As the aircraft encounters a headwind, the headwind opposes the aircraft's speed, and as the aircraft flies with the flow of air, a tailwind, it aids the speed of the aircraft.

The next illustrations shows the shearing action of changing wind direction which affects the flight of the aircraft. As the aircraft flies from a headwind into a region of a tailwind (shearing), it will cause the aircraft to descend, or pitch downward. If the aircraft flies from a tailwind into a region of a headwind (shearing) it will cause the aircraft to ascend, or pitch upward. Thus, the shearing action of opposite winds influences both the direction, pitch (up or down), and the speed of the aircraft for a short distance.

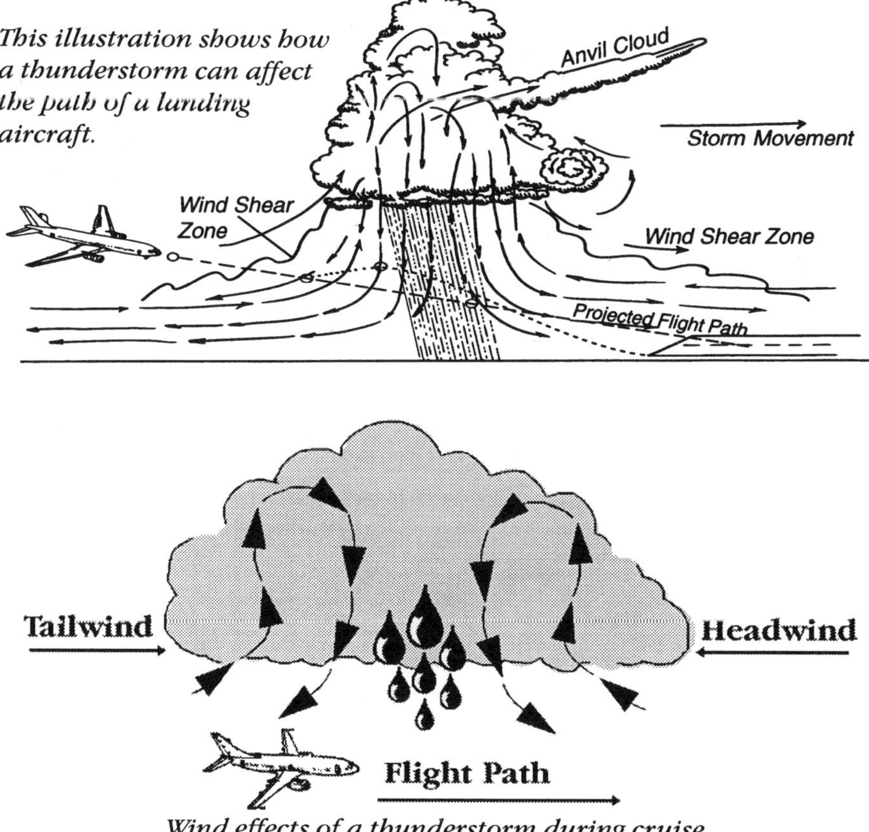

Wind effects of a thunderstorm during cruise.

Because windshear is more prevalent in certain regions due to thunderstorm activity or mountainous terrain, the airports within these regions are equipped with windshear detectors. These detectors are located in various areas on the airport. Should there be windshear in the airport area, the detectors will forward the information to the Control Tower and the Control Tower will advise aircraft on the ground, as well as in the air. The Control Tower will also update the Automatic Terminal Information Service (ATIS) (see page 26) with the windshear advisory.

In addition to airports having a windshear detection system, most airline jets are equipped with a very similar windshear detection system.

When the Pilots go through their semi-annual training, as part of the training program, the Pilots will (at a minimum) experience simulated windshear on an Approach, a Landing, a Take-Off, and a Departure. The reason for this, as in all other emergency exercises performed, is that if an emergency occurs, it's like "old hat" to the Pilots.

De-Ice/Anti-Ice

With the right combination of temperature and moisture in the air, the aircraft, whether it is on the ground or in the air, can accumulate ice. Should this occur on the ground while the aircraft is at the gate, the Pilots have a few choices. Depending on the airport de-icing facilities, the aircraft may get de-iced at the gate, away from the gate, and in some cases, minutes prior to take-off.

Regardless of the de-ice location, some common procedures will take place. The Pilots normally make an announcement about the need for de-icing, and perhaps a brief description of the procedure. You may notice that the air conditioning system will temporarily be turned off to decrease the odor of the de-icing fluid. If you have a sensitive nose and can detect the odor, rest assured it will not last long.

Speaking of being temporary, the de-ice/anti-ice fluid has an expiration time. Depending on the type of fluid used, it can last up to 1½ hours. Once airborne, it's usually a matter of minutes before the aircraft is out of icing conditions.

If the time has expired, the First Officer (usually) or Flight Engineer will come through the cabin to perform a visual inspection of the wings prior to take-off to determine if a second de-ice is required. In addition to this, the Ground Crew (depending on the location) will inspect the aircraft.

Let's talk about what occurs in the air when icing, freezing rain, or snow exists.

The Pilots become aware of icing, freezing rain, or snow that exists along the route from receiving printed weather data, by observing cloud formations and the temperature at the altitude they're flying, and from other aircraft which may have encountered it preceding them. With all of this knowledge, the Pilots know when to use the aircraft's anti-icing and de-icing systems. These systems utilize the hot air produced by the engines and route it via a ducting system, to parts of the wings and engines. Electrical power also aids in de-icing and anti-icing for the flight deck windows and certain outside probes used for instrument indications. Also of interest, in addition to heating the windows to prevent icing, the heat improves the impact strength of the windows, in the event of birds hitting the aircraft windows.

Before the Pilots land, either the tower or the recorded weather data, Automatic Terminal Information Service (ATIS) (see page 26) will tell what the expected braking action is on the runway in use. With this information, the Pilots can determine if it's safe to land, and if so, they can adjust their landing point and the use of thrust reversers as well as auto brakes (if installed) and plan where the aircraft should exit the runway onto the taxiway. All this is a consideration when you're dealing with a slick runway. Remember, they're professionals and have years of experience.

Mechanical

Repairs must take place before the aircraft is allowed to leave. We hope that passengers will be patient, since their safety comes first. Some minor "write-ups" can be deferred for repair, if it does not affect the safety of the flight and/or safety of the passengers.

All write-ups are checked in an aircraft manual to determine which status that they fall under.

Sometimes an aircraft that has just landed is scheduled to leave in 30 minutes. Something as simple as a lavatory light not working can delay the flight because a mechanic will have to determine whether it's a bad bulb, relay, or light assembly, etc., which takes a minute or two. After determining the cause, they have to determine if it can be repaired in a timely manner, or if they must close off or restrict the use of the lavatory for safety reasons. It is possible to have a mechanical delay the last 10 minutes before pushback (when you leave the gate). But keep in mind that the aircraft probably has only been on the ground for 20 minutes. During this time passengers disembark, the Pilot picks up new flight paperwork, cleaners come onto the plane, catering and fueling occurs, and of course, your boarding, to mention a few of the things going on in that short time.

Once again, we know that you want to get to your destination on time—but your safety must come first.

Last-Minute Details

Now that you're walking down the jetway onto the aircraft, you'll probably look at your ticket once again and check your seat assignment. After that you may look into the flight deck/cockpit and see the Pilots reviewing paper work. This paper work usually consists of a flight plan, a fuel slip, departure route charts, weather charts, and a checklist. And that's just the *basic* paperwork!

Some airlines have the paperwork sent by a computer before departure. The Pilots take all of the information from the paper-work or computer, put it into a flight computer, and/or use it to calculate the aircraft performance—how much can we weigh to make a safe take off in the event of an engine failure? All take off performance is, believe it or not, based on the risk of an engine failure—which is good if you think about it. We'll discuss this more in the chapter on take-offs.

The flight deck, also known as the cockpit, is available for viewing while the aircraft is at the gate and a Pilot is present. All you need to do is request a visit from the Pilot or Flight Attendant, and time permitting, it's not a problem. This is available for all ages, and it's been known to have a calming effect for some passengers by taking some of the mystery out of flying and being able to meet your Pilots.

When you find your seat and you are ready to go, you may see some last minute changes. Cargo or standby passengers often must catch the next flight because the outside temperature rises in the summer, especially in the desert or high altitudes which causes a weight take-off issue. This may seem to be an inconvenience to you at the time, but you certainly will rest assured knowing that your aircraft will take-off safely because of these changes.

Weight Evaluated

You may wonder how will the heavy aircraft fly? With a lot of thrust on a good day, and on a not-so-good day (high tempera-tures, high elevation, heavy weight, etc.) some changes must take place.

On a hot day passengers and/or baggage will be a consider-ation, so the aircraft may take-off at ¾ full on a normally sold out flight, because it needs to be lighter to lift off. The reason for this is, even if the aircraft is using full thrust, the density of the air requires a longer take-off roll to reach the speed needed to lift off and maintain a safe climbout, in the event of an engine problem.

Although the performance data is checked on all departures, the departure weight is more critical in warmer temperatures and higher elevations. This effect is similar to a heavy car going uphill on a warm day or uphill in high elevations. The lighter it is, the easier it is to climb. All airlines do consider weight and temperature restrictions.

Automatic Terminal Information Services

After the Pilots receive the paperwork for the flight and have performed the walk-around inspection, they will get the local weather information, which has critical information concerning field conditions, departure runways in use, weather, temperature (which affects take off/landing performance), visibility, and if there are any gate holds. This automatic weather information is called ATIS, which stands for Automatic Terminal Information Service.

All this information is recorded and is updated at least once an hour—sometimes sooner if there are weather changes or runway changes due to storms or wind shifts in the area.

Auxiliary Power Unit

Have you ever seen the fumes and exhaust coming from the tail section of an aircraft and wondered what it is?

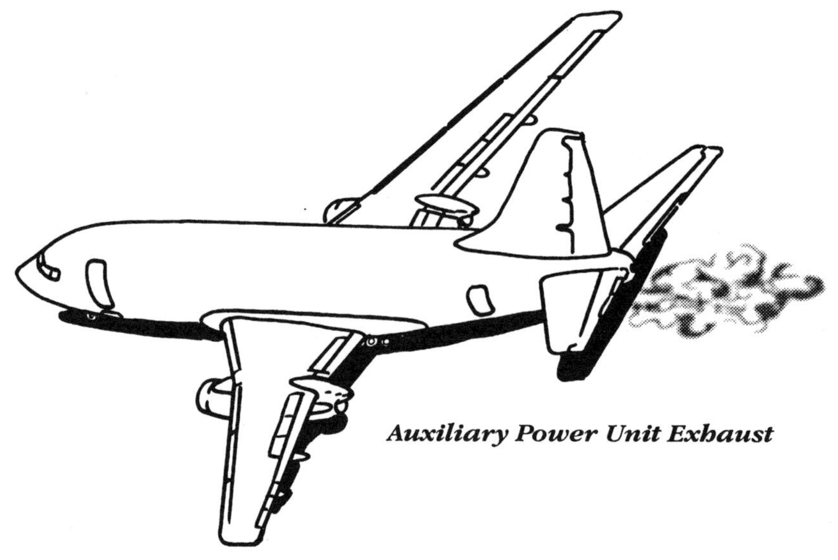

Auxiliary Power Unit Exhaust

Well, most commercial jet aircraft have an additional jet engine located in the tail section. This engine is called the Auxiliary Power Unit (APU). It does not provide thrust as the aircraft's main engines do. The purpose of the APU is to provide compressed air and/or electrical power to the aircraft.

The APU is used on the ground to supply electrical power to the aircraft systems if the engines are not running and the airport power carts are not available. Also, the compressed air can be used for ground air conditioning while the engines are not running. Because the APU isn't as large and powerful as the main engines, the amount of air flow will be less than when the main engines are supplying the air conditioning.

The air produced from the APU is what is used to start the aircraft engines normally. If the APU is unusable, then the airport provides an air cart in which a hose is connected to the aircraft to produce the air needed to start the engine.

The APU is used in the air as a backup for the electrical power and/or air conditioning. The APU can operate the entire essential electrical systems without any interruption, should there be a failure of normal electrical power. If you should have an engine failure, this is one additional back-up.

Push-back (or power-back) is when the aircraft leaves the gate. For your comfort, it would be wise to attend to any physiological needs (ideally in the terminal) prior to push-back. Delays in departure or turbulence in-flight could cause the seatbelt sign to stay on, and you may not be able to move about the cabin and access the bathrooms immediately, or perhaps even for the entire flight, due to turbulence.

Once you find your seat location, please reserve the floor space in front of your feet <u>for your feet</u>. It is so very important you keep this area clear in the event of an evacuation. Just ask the person seated next to the window how important it is. Also, it is very important that your seatback is in the locked and upright position during take-off and landing, in case of an emergency evacuation. The passenger seated behind you could be greatly delayed in an evacuation of the aircraft if your seatback is not in the upright position. Please think about it.

Now that you're seated, hoping the seat next to you remains empty, you may look around you to see how you can get comfortable. The seasoned passenger knows to get a pillow and blanket from the overhead compartment, and open the air vent. If you need any assistance, just ask the Flight Attendant.

Finally, when you feel comfortable and the air is flowing, it's time to leave the gate. Your loved ones watching from the airport will know this is about to occur when the red rotating beacon light on the top and bottom of the aircraft is turned on. This signals the ground crew that the aircraft is about to start engines and push-back from the gate.

Interruption of Air Conditioning

Just when you have the air-conditioning vent just right, all of a sudden the airflow slows to almost nil.

What's happening is that when the aircraft is push-backed, the Pilot starts the engines. To do this the Pilot needs the air supply that also supplies your vent for a minute or two to aid in starting the engine. Normally after an engine is started, the Pilot will return that nice airflow you had established.

Safety Announcements

By now the Flight Attendants are demonstrating the aircraft safety features. It's very important that you listen for the 3 minutes or so, because they are giving you instructions in how to prepare yourself in the event of an emergency. After you listen and understand what you can do to help yourself, then you will have the confidence to help someone who may not have listened. Have you ever wondered what the phrases *"Prepare Doors"* or *"Flight Attendants, prepare your doors and cross-check"* mean? Well the Flight Attendants, before leaving the gate, set all exit doors on the aircraft by arming the escape slide for automatic deployment. They also place the colored strap across the exit door window so the ground personnel will not reopen the door until knocking on the aircraft door or notifying the Flight Crew . It would be quite noticeable if the door was opened after being armed—not only would the slide inflate, you would be delayed for an hour or two. Since there is at least one Flight Attendant per two exit doors, they will check one door and turn around and check the other one, hence *"cross check"*.

One Engine Taxi Due to a Long Line of Departing Aircraft, or Long Taxi

Sometimes when the Pilots push-back they may only start one engine of a two-engine jet, because the Pilot anticipates a long taxi or a delay in departure. By having one engine shut down, it reduces fuel burn as well as unnecessary noise and pollutants. So don't be concerned if you hear only one engine start. However, it can be necessary to start all engines due to the weight of the aircraft.

After push-back and engine start, while the Flight Attendants are performing the safety demonstrations, the Pilots are getting clearance to taxi to the active runway, selecting the proper flap position for the take-off, and performing their taxi checklist. At this time, you may notice the cabin lights blink off and back on again as the aircraft power source has been transferred from the APU to the engine generators.

Seatbelts

Let's talk about seatbelts. Now you know how important it is to have it buckled before push-back and also in the air, but why is it important after landing?

Did you know as you're taxiing in after landing, the same ground personnel, including ramp personnel, baggage handlers, ground supervisors, and even aircraft either taxiing in or out, are all moving about before and after you land? Not to mention animals— yes, animals—that can run in front of an aircraft causing the Pilots to stop the aircraft suddenly to keep from hitting them or having aircraft damage. At some airports, there may be places where animals can get on the airport property and eventually access the runway and taxiway area.

It is also very important to have your seatbelt fastened in the air. Even scattered clouds can produce turbulence. In addition, clear air turbulence (CAT) can be caused from converging air masses, strong winds around mountainous areas, and area storms, to mention a few.

Clear air turbulence can be very violent. Although it is rare, when it does occur, those passengers who don't have their seatbelts on can become airborne within the aircraft, which can cause multiple broken bones or even more serious injuries.

The Pilots can only react after the initial impact because clear air turbulence is just that—clear air, which is not detectable until encountered. Consequently, those passengers who did not heed the multiple announcements: "Please keep your seatbelts fastened about you in the event of unexpected turbulence," may place themselves and others at risk.

Also, don't forget about that aircraft that took off 2 minutes before yours. The aircraft's wake can be thought of as similar to the wake of a boat going across the lake. It produces waves on the water as an aircraft will in the air. And because the Pilots can't see "waves in the air", you can be caught off guard by choppy air. This is discussed in more detail in the next chapter.

These facts and reasons are why so many airlines state repeatedly: "While you're seated, at all times, please check and make sure your seatbelts are securely fastened about you." After all, it is *about you!*

Zero To Zoom

When the aircraft is established on the runway and cleared for take-off, the Pilots advance the power 1/4 to 1/3 of the take-off power and wait for the engines to stabilize or "spool up" together. Sometimes they take 1 to 3 seconds to stabilize.

If the full take-off power was set initially and one of the engines were lagging, the aircraft would have a tendency to veer to the left or right. Also, by allowing the engines to stabilize, the Pilots are able to check the engine instruments and various other gauges to make sure they're in "the green" or within limitations. Once this is established, the remaining take-off power is set. At this time you may feel and hear the runway centerline lights as the nose wheel rolls over them. It sounds like your car on the freeway when you change lanes, only a little bit louder. The same sound can be felt and heard on landing, but at a higher speed.

As the aircraft is increasing speed down the runway and the Pilots are monitoring their instruments, they have a set speed, increasing to "V_1." or Velocity 1. If a malfunction occurs prior to this speed, the aircraft can safely reject the take-off and still have enough runway remaining to stop safely. If a malfunction occurs at or after this speed, the Pilots will continue the take-off, because performance data indicates that there is not enough runway to stop the aircraft safely on the remaining runway.

After take-off, the gear is retracted at approximately 100 feet above the ground. In smaller aircraft (Boeing 737, DC9, MD80) you may hear and/or feel the nose gear as it slows it's rotation speed against a stopper, known as a "snubber".

When reaching 1,000 feet above the ground, most airlines will reduce the take-off thrust to a climb thrust, since the take-off critical stage is over, and you do not need the full power. After you reach 1,000 feet, the Pilots will lower the nose, to increase speed and start retracting the flaps, as you may hear and see on the wings. You may feel turbulence caused by a previously departing aircraft's wake.

This wake is caused by the difference in air pressure on top and bottom of the wing as the aircraft is flying. The air pressure on top of the wing is a low pressure, and the air passing under the wing is a high pressure. This is what creates lift. The by-product of this is known as wing-tip vortices.

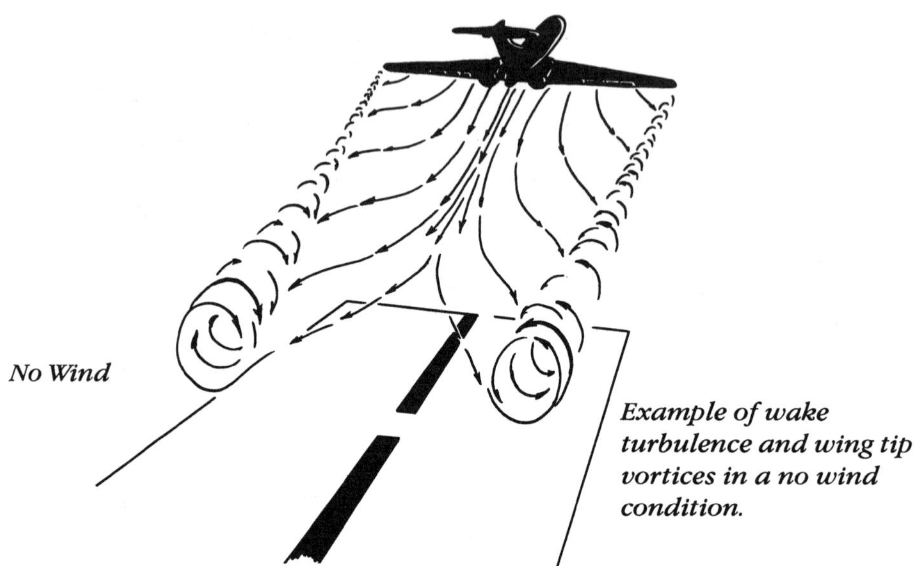

No Wind

Example of wake turbulence and wing tip vortices in a no wind condition.

When the two air masses meet at the tip of the wing it produces a swirling effect similar to a horizontal tornado, but with less force and trails behind the aircraft for a few minutes, depending on the wind conditions at the airport.

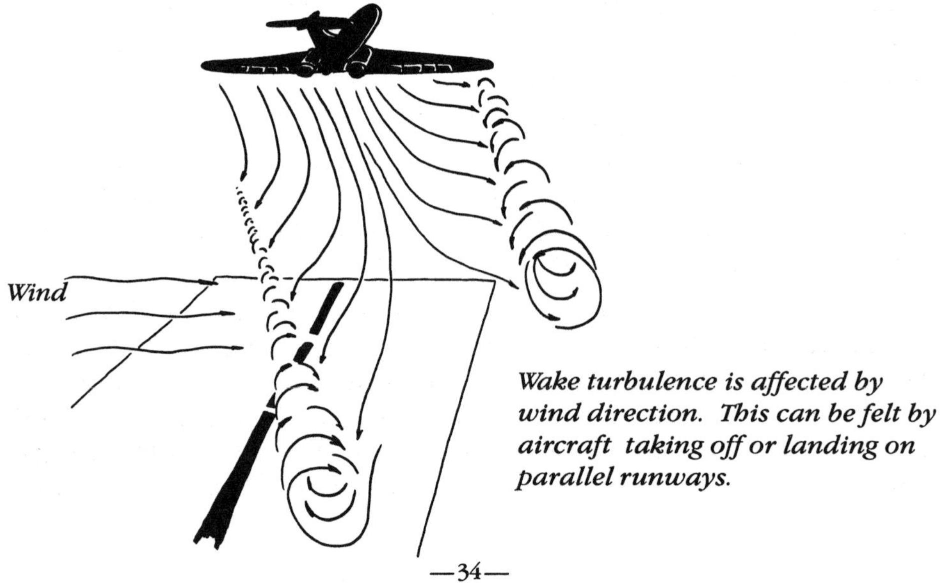

Wind

Wake turbulence is affected by wind direction. This can be felt by aircraft taking off or landing on parallel runways.

As the aircraft size, shape, and weight increase, so do the wing tip vortices in size and strength. This is one of the reasons why the arrivals and departures are delayed or timed. Even with timing and distance behind the previous aircraft, these vortices may linger, and you may feel a "bump" or two as your flight passes through the remaining vortices.

Another factor that can cause turbulence in lower altitudes is uneven heating of the earth, also known as convective currents.

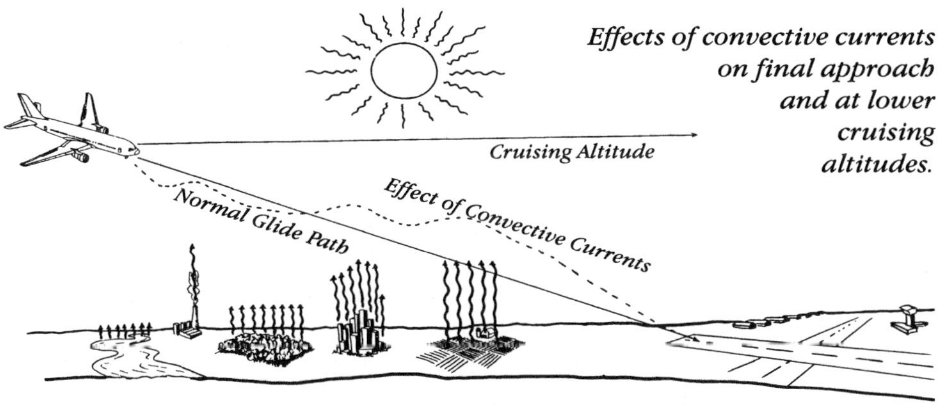

It is from sun warming the ground surface. When you have a bare area next to trees or even buildings, heat absorption is at a different rate, so as the heat rises from the surface it is uneven, therefore causing up and down drafts. This can be more noticeable in desert regions, or mountainous areas.

As the aircraft climbs or descends from the surface to 10,000 feet, there is an FAA rule that requires a "Sterile Cockpit", which means that the Pilots are so busy that they cannot be disturbed, unless it is an absolute emergency. This is the critical stage of flight because the Pilots are busy climbing or descending, turning, talking with approach or departure control, and looking for other aircraft. These are just a few of the things Pilots are doing during this important time of the flight.

The Flight Attendants are notified by chimes, bells, or other ways, depending on the airline, when climbing through 10,000 feet. This is their indication that it is permissible for the Flight Attendants to contact the Pilots over normal situations. It is then safe for the Flight Attendants to move about the cabin unless the Captain has instructed the Flight Attendants to remain seated after the 10,000 foot signal due to adverse weather conditions.

Should an emergency arise prior to 10,000 feet when climbing, the Flight Attendant will assist you, and if needed, notify the Pilots. The same applies when descending through 10,000 feet. You may hear the Flight Attendant state "The Captain has indicated we are on our final descent . . . ."

Departure

Just as you have many turns and different speed limits when you're driving from the city to the freeway, airlines departing from the same city have very similar rules. In addition to the turns and speed changes, the airlines also work with altitude rules or limits when joining their freeway in the air. This is known to Pilots as an airway.

Because there aren't any signs in the air, the airlines use specific departure routes, by following Departure Procedures. The Departure Procedure has specific turns, speeds and altitude restrictions, depending on the direction the jet is headed. A Departure Procedure, also known as a "DP", is used by all carriers and most large airports. If a DP is not used, radar vectors or an assigned heading (or direction) will be used to connect to the in-route chart. This usually is from take-off to approximately 25,000 feet, or about 80 miles away from the airport. This keeps the departure traffic separated from the arrival traffic. We'll study the arrival procedure in the Arrivals chapter. Let's look at a Departure Procedure.

On the following page is a DP for Phoenix Sky Harbor Airport, called the Drake Six.

This departure is used when the aircraft is headed north toward Las Vegas, Los Angeles, Sacramento, Reno, and other destinations.

By looking at this picture, you'll see probably more than you want to know; however, let's look at a few things:

First, locate the runways. You'll see them in the lower center of the picture. Now if you look to the left and right of the runways, you'll see on the departure the combination of altitude (in this case 3,000 feet) and mileage, which is represented by the letters DME (Distance Measuring Equipment). This is similar to what's indicated by an odometer in a car.

DRAKE SIX DEPARTURE (DRK6.DRK) (PILOT NAV)
(RESTRICTED TO TURBOJET AND TURBOPROP AIRCRAFT)
(DME REQUIRED) (RADAR REQUIRED)

This SID requires minimum climb gradients of:
Rwys 8L/R: After PXR VOR, 380' per NM
to 7000'.
Rwys 26L/R: After PXR 4 DME, 390' per NM
to 7000'.

Gnd speed-Kts	75	100	150	200	250	300
380' per NM	475	633	950	1267	1583	1900
390' per NM	488	650	975	1300	1625	1950

TAKE-OFF

Rwy 8L: Climb via a 085° heading to intercept and proceed via PXR R-075. Cross PXR R-350 at or below 3000'. At D4 East of PXR VOR turn LEFT to a 020° heading. At 13 DME turn LEFT to a 300° heading to intercept the PXR R-336 to Maier Int. Thence via DRK R-127 to DRK VOR.

Rwy 8R: Proceed direct PXR VOR, thence via PXR R-075, cross PXR VOR at or below 3000'. At D4 East of PXR VOR turn LEFT to a 020° heading. At 13 DME turn LEFT to a 300° heading to intercept the PXR R-336 to Maier Int. Thence via DRK R-127 to DRK VOR.

Rwys 26L/R: Climb via runway heading or via heading assigned by ATC. Cross 4 DME West of PXR VOR at or below 3000'. At 9 DME West of PXR VOR turn RIGHT to a 360° heading to intercept PXR R-336 to Maier Int. Thence via DRK R-127 to DRK VOR.

<u>Expect</u> filed altitude 3 minutes after departure.

Direct distance from Phoenix Sky Harbor Intl to:
Banyo Int **24 NM**
Maier Int **63 NM**

Not for Navigational Use

**Reproduced with permission of
Jeppesen Sanderson, Inc.**

PHOENIX Departure (R) 119.2

DRAKE SIX DEPARTURE (DRK6.DRK) (PILOT NAV)
(RESTRICTED TO TURBOJET AND TURBOPROP AIRCRAFT)
(DME REQUIRED) (RADAR REQUIRED)

This SID requires minimum climb gradients of:
Rwys 8L/R: After PXR VOR, 380' per NM to 7000'.
Rwys 26L/R: After PXR 4 DME, 390' per NM to 7000'.

Gnd speed-Kts	75	100	150	200	250	300
380' per NM	475	633	950	1267	1583	1900
390' per NM	488	650	975	1300	1625	1950

TAKE-OFF

Rwy 8L: Climb via a 085° heading to intercept and proceed via PXR R-075. Cross PXR R-350 at or below 3000'. At D4 East of PXR VOR turn LEFT to a 020° heading. At 13 DME turn LEFT to a 300° heading to intercept the PXR R-336 to Maier Int. Thence via DRK R-127 to DRK VOR.

Rwy 8R: Proceed direct PXR VOR, thence via PXR R-075, cross PXR VOR at or below 3000'. At D4 East of PXR VOR turn LEFT to a 020° heading. At 13 DME turn LEFT to a 300° heading to intercept the PXR R-336 to Maier Int. Thence via DRK R-127 to DRK VOR.

Rwys 26L/R: Climb via runway heading or via heading assigned by ATC. Cross 4 DME West of PXR VOR at or below 3000'. At 9 DME West of PXR VOR turn RIGHT to a 360° heading to intercept PXR R-336 to Maier Int. Thence via DRK R-127 to DRK VOR.

Expect filed altitude 3 minutes after departure.

Direct distance from Phoenix Sky Harbor Intl to:
Banyo Int **24 NM**
Maier Int **63 NM**

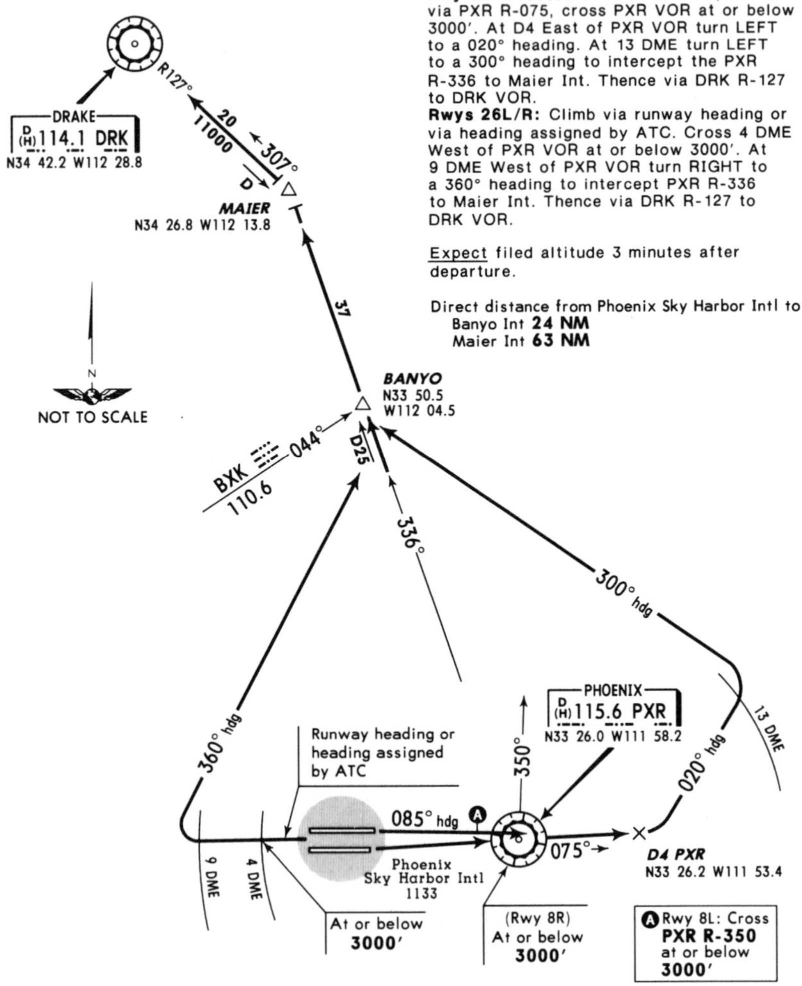

Not for Navigational Use

Reproduced with permission of
Jeppesen Sanderson, Inc.

Going to the left of the runway, you'll be at or below 3,000 feet until 4 miles, then continue to climb to your assigned altitude. When you get to 9 miles, you turn right to a heading of north (or 360°) until 25 miles. That's it! Now you join or intercept the rest of your departure. Remember, it's all altitude, mileage, and turns. *Piece of cake!*

The degree of involvement depends on the direction of flight and the airport.

While you're at your cruise altitude, you may have several questions that you want to ask the Pilots or Flight Attendants. I hope in this chapter that I can answer some of those questions for you.

Pressure Changes

Have you ever wondered why your ears "pop" when you're in an airplane? As the aircraft leaves the gate the Pilots start the pressurization process. This will slowly start pressurizing the aircraft, so by the time the aircraft has reached it's final cruising altitude your body is comfortable.

Because most jets climb between 1,000-3,000 feet per minute, it is necessary to start pressurizing the cabin prior to take-off. By the time the aircraft reaches the final cruising altitude the cabin will be pressurized to approximately 5,500 feet. (This figure may vary at higher altitudes.)

The pressurization effect is similar to a car traveling from sea level up to the mountains. The air pressure decreases as the terrain increases. Because the eardrum is affected by the pressure change, the Eustachian tube (which connects the middle ear to the nasopharynx) allows the air pressure inside the ear to be equal to the outside air pressure. Sometimes a "pop" sound may be heard. While traveling on the ground to a higher elevation, the "popping" may not be as noticeable because of the slow change in pressure.

The pressurization effect is the same on descent. That is, the Eustachian tube is trying to equalize the pressure difference. There are times your ears may "pop" during cruise because it may be necessary to change altitudes due to weather conditions or a request from the Air Traffic Controllers. When the Air Traffic Controllers request the aircraft to stay at a lower final altitude than the aircraft was originally pressurized for, the pilots will have to adjust the pressurization for the new final altitude, which may also affect your ears.

Because of the pressure changes in the aircraft and in the ears, it can be quite painful to travel with a cold since the congestion or blockage in your Eustachian tubes prevents the Eustachian tubes from equalizing the pressure.

Swallowing, yawning, or chewing gum may help open the Eustachian tubes and allow the pressure to equalize. This is why infants usually start crying before take-off and landing. It's always recommended that a bottle or pacifier be given to encourage them to swallow and equalize their tiny ears.

Cabin Temperature

Have you ever been so cold that eventually you ask the Flight Attendant for a blanket? Well, did you know that most commercial jets have two air-conditioning units? Approximately 70% of one unit goes to the Flight Deck, with the remainder going to the cabin. The majority of the Flight Deck air conditioning is routed through the electronic equipment area. This keeps the aircraft computers and flight instruments from overheating. 100% of the second unit goes into the cabin.

In the Flight Deck, there is one thermostat to independently adjust the temperature on each unit. Now the Pilots are comfortable, and they try to make you comfortable by setting the thermostats appropriate to the number of passengers on board. Well, sometimes it needs to be adjusted, and guess what—if you, the passenger, don't say anything, the Pilots think you're comfortable. Don't freeze in silence. Please tell the Flight Attendant to relay the message about the temperature.

Keep in mind that in the summer months, it does take a while to cool down an aircraft, so please be patient. As the aircraft climbs out, it will cool down. Just think of it as your hot car trying to cool down. It's not going to be instantaneous.

Aircraft Speed

Aircraft air speed vs. aircraft ground speed: Have you been on the airplane wondering what it means when the Pilots say in their announcement, "Today we have a ground speed of . . . ?" On your flight before this one, that aircraft was going 100 miles per hour faster, and it's the same size aircraft, and you're wondering just how can it vary so much?

There are several causes for the speed difference. Let's look at the term "aircraft air speed." The aircraft air speed is just that—how fast the aircraft is capable of flying under it's own power across the sky, similar to a motor boat moving across a calm lake. For instance, consider the chart on the next page.

Boeing 737-200 Boeing 737-300 Boeing 737-400	Average cruise speed between 530-575 miles per hour
Boeing 757	Average cruise speed between 560-581 miles per hour
Boeing 747	Average cruise speed between 564-583 miles per hour
DC9 MD80 MD90	Average cruise speed 565 miles per hour

The aircraft's weight and type of engines can affect the aircraft's air speed.

If we take the aircraft's actual speed and add the high level altitude winds, we will have what is known as the aircraft ground speed, or how fast the aircraft is moving across the ground.

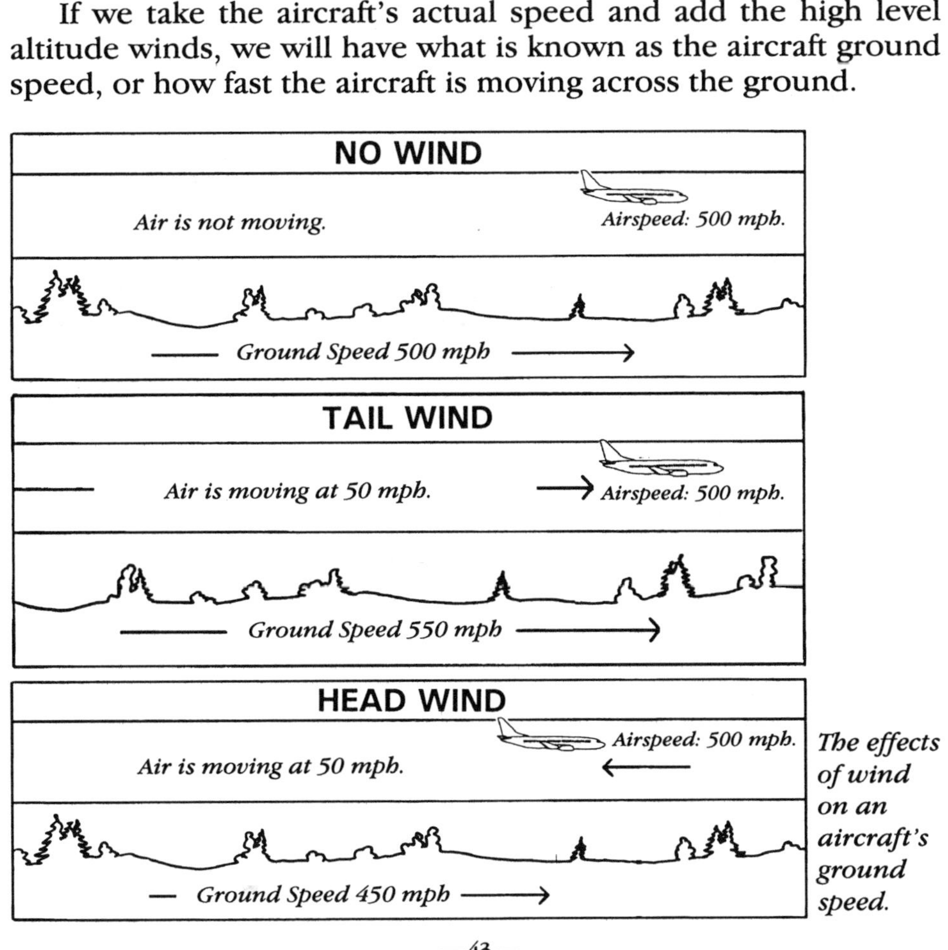

The effects of wind on an aircraft's ground speed.

The high altitude winds which are responsible for moving the storm systems across the globe also play a significant part in moving an aircraft across the globe.

These same winds can increase or decrease the ground speed, depending upon which direction the aircraft is flying. The upper altitude winds usually move from the west toward the east. In addition, there can be what is known as a jetstream.

A jetstream is a swift high altitude "river" of air (75-250 miles per hour) that moves generally from the west to the east and moves accordingly with the season, north and south.

Similar to a river, the center of the jetstream has the highest velocity. As the distance from the center increases, the velocity decreases, such as along the river bank where the current is slower.

The airlines may utilize the jetstream in a safe manner by planning the route of the aircraft accordingly, with the aircraft going eastbound, for a more positive ground speed, and avoiding the jetstream for the aircraft going westbound, as much as possible.

Making Up Time

What about the infamous question, can you make up time? Well, most of the time, yes. However, at least three things have to occur. One, the Pilots will request direct routing with the Air Traffic Controllers, and depending upon the jet traffic, the Controllers will accommodate them; two, the Pilots will increase the speed of the aircraft, provided there is additional fuel; and three, if special airspace (i.e., for military operations, alert areas, restricted airspace, national security areas, etc.) is not being used if the more direct routing infringes on it.

Where Are We?

How many times have you wondered, "Where are we?" I guarantee you the Pilots know where they are, you just have to ask where you are! As the Pilots cruise across the cities and the states, they are using their instruments in conjunction with ground radio signals. These ground stations are called Very High Frequency Omni-Directional Range Stations, also called VORS. Most all airports have one of the facilities on the field or nearby, in addition to VORS in remote places.

The Pilots use these VORS to go from Point A to Point B. It is possible in some aircraft to navigate by connecting a latitude and longitude point and flying directly to this point. This is known as a waypoint. So you may see a city below you and the Pilots know of it by a latitude/longitude point. If you ask "What was that city?", it may take a minute longer to answer your question versus if the Pilots were flying by means of the VORS.

Speed Changes

Why is the aircraft slowing down and not descending? There can be several reasons. At peak hours of travel, the sky can get congested, and to prevent holding, the Pilots are requested by Air Traffic Controllers to slow down to a set or assigned air speed.

Another reason is reports of turbulence ahead of the aircraft. If the plane slows down, it won't be as choppy. Of course, the other choice is to fly at a different altitude, provided reports of smooth air exist and other jet traffic isn't present.

Contrails

What are those white streaks in the air?

The simple explanation: Have you ever been outside when the temperature is very cold and noticed when you exhale, you see your breath? The same thing is happening to a jet. If the temperature is cold enough at the jet's altitude, you'll see the engine's "breath".

The expanded explanation: When the jet's fuel is burned, it produces a by-product called heated hydrogen. When this heated hydrogen is mixed with the atmosphere's oxygen it forms water vapor, or condensation. If the temperature is cold enough, this condensation freezes, which leaves a trail behind the aircraft which is known as a condensation trail or "contrail".

Approaches

Airport Arrivals or STARs.

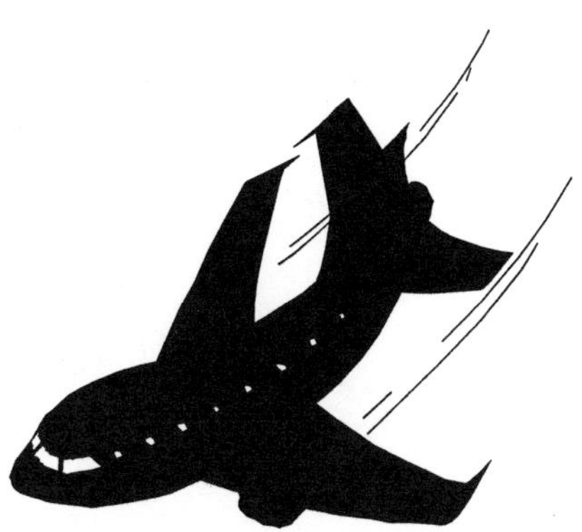

The airport arrival procedures, also known as Standard Terminal Arrival Routes (STARs), are very similar to the departure procedures, because they're both based on turns, altitudes, and speed limits. There is one difference—remember how, in the previous diagrams, you located the airport runways first on the departure and followed the arrows out away from the runway? Well, for the airport arrivals, do just the opposite—start at the sides, top or bottom of the next diagrams and follow the arrows toward the runways.

As the two diagrams on page 48 and 49 show, some arrivals can be very simple and others more complicated. It also depends on the airport and if that particular arrival is available for inbound aircraft from several directions.

Let's compare the two arrivals into Los Angeles. On the Civet Four arrival, if you look to the far right or top of the picture, then follow the arrows toward the runway, you'll become familiar again with the distance and altitude restrictions. The distance will be represented by the letter D or DME.

Look under the word Civet (at the upper left of the diagram), and you'll see D52 ILAX. The distance from that point to Los Angeles International Airport (ILAX) is 52 miles. Now follow the arrow to the next point, Bremr D40/12,000 feet. On this arrival, the aircraft will be at an altitude of 12,000 feet 40 miles away from the airport. With the next lower altitude at Arnes D33/11,000 feet, and so on. Good job!

Now let's look at the other arrival into Los Angeles called the Downe Four. Wow! Remember the basics—arrows inbound to the runway, altitude, turns, and speed restrictions. Just take one point of arrival and work with the information you've been given. See? It's not as complicated as it first appears.

D-ATIS Arrival **133.8**

CIVET FOUR ARRIVAL (CIVET.CIVET4)
(RADAR OR DME REQUIRED)

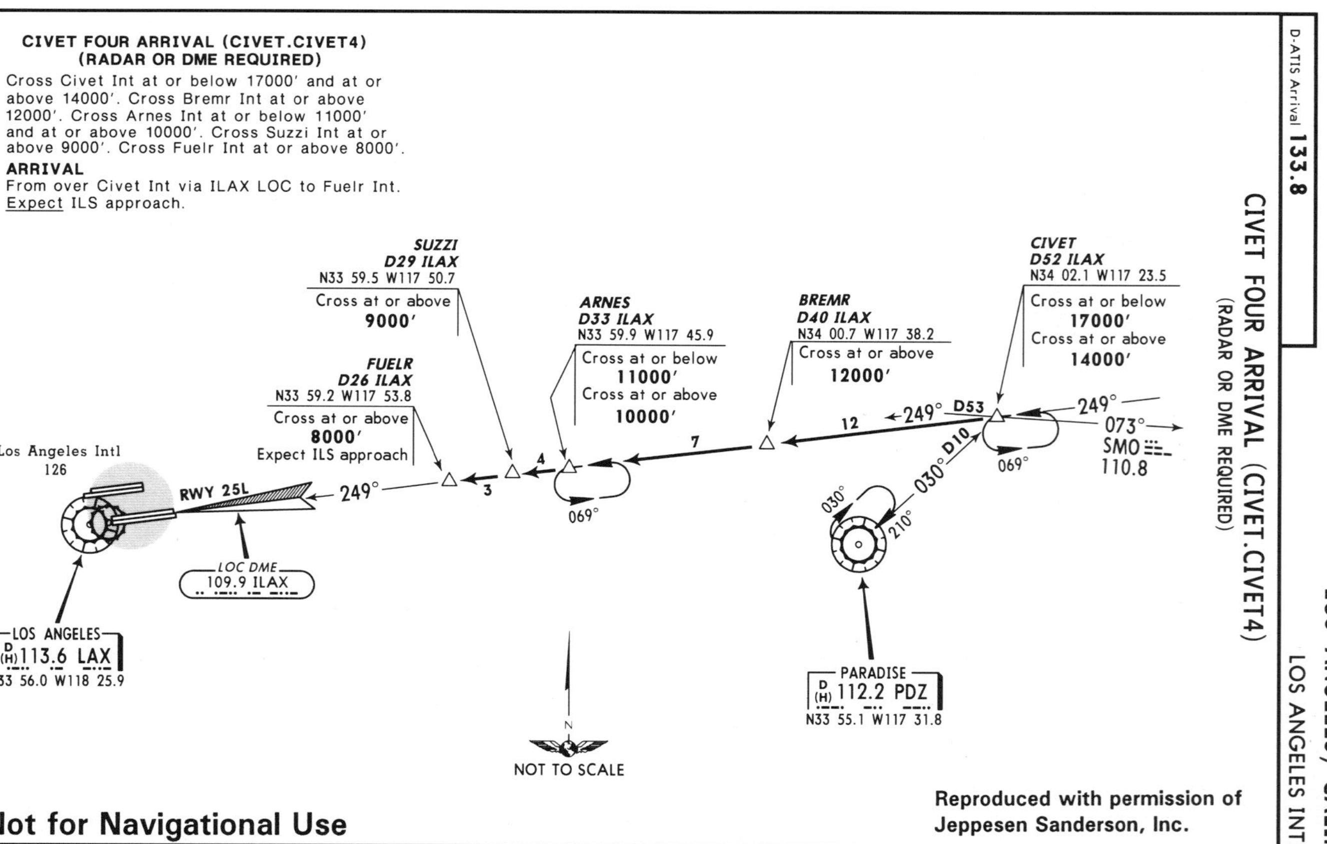

DOWNE FOUR ARRIVAL (DOWNE.DOWNE4)
(ARRIVAL UTILIZED FOR NOISE ABATEMENT BETWEEN 0000 LT AND 0630 LT)
(DME REQUIRED)

Not for Navigational Use

Reproduced with permission of Jeppesen Sanderson, Inc.

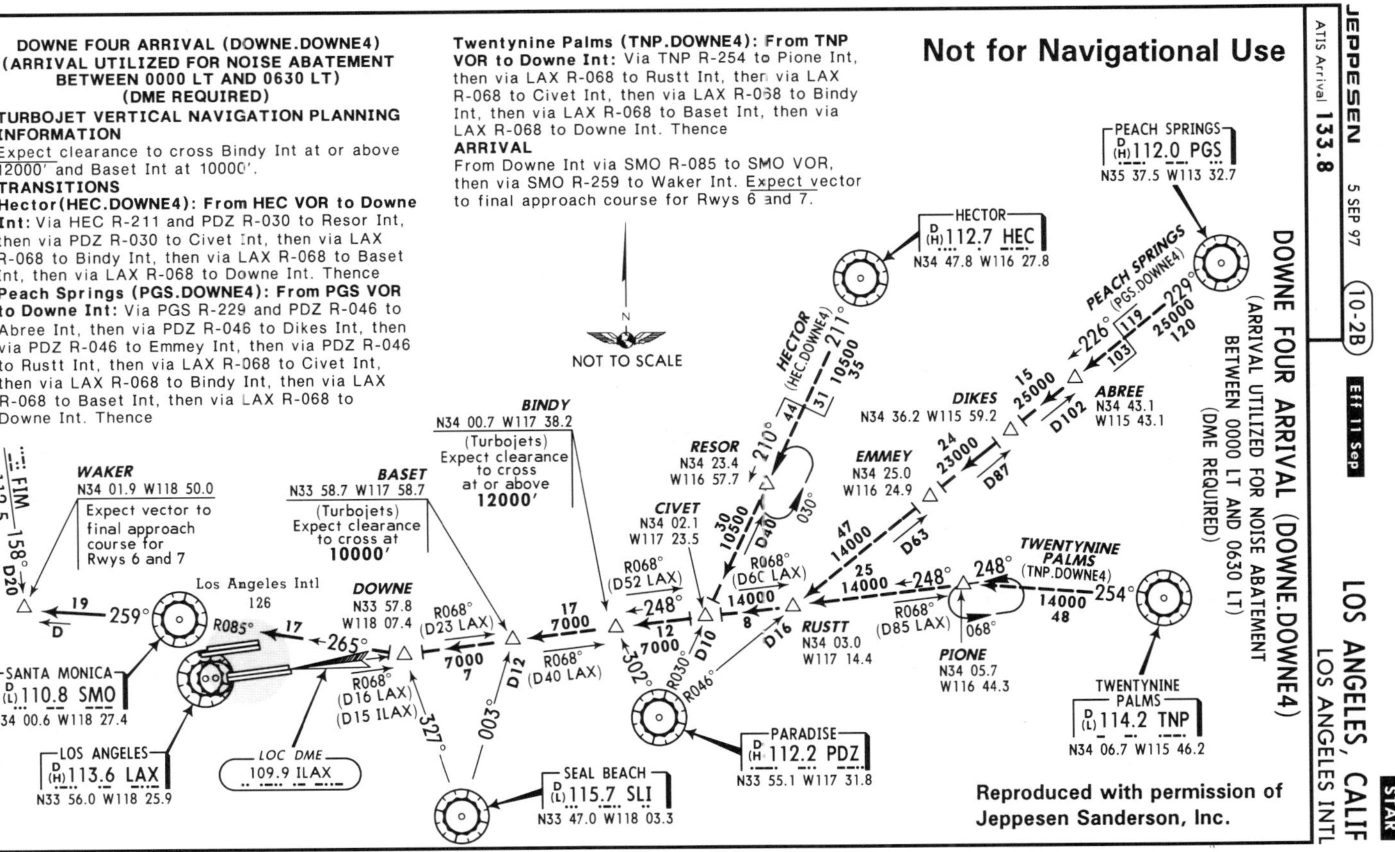

DOWNE FOUR ARRIVAL (DOWNE.DOWNE4)
(ARRIVAL UTILIZED FOR NOISE ABATEMENT BETWEEN 0000 LT AND 0630 LT)
(DME REQUIRED)

TURBOJET VERTICAL NAVIGATION PLANNING INFORMATION

Expect clearance to cross Bindy Int at or above 12000' and Baset Int at 10000'.

TRANSITIONS

Hector (HEC.DOWNE4): From HEC VOR to Downe Int: Via HEC R-211 and PDZ R-030 to Resor Int, then via PDZ R-030 to Civet Int, then via LAX R-068 to Bindy Int, then via LAX R-068 to Baset Int, then via LAX R-068 to Downe Int. Thence

Peach Springs (PGS.DOWNE4): From PGS VOR to Downe Int: Via PGS R-229 and PDZ R-046 to Abree Int, then via PDZ R-046 to Dikes Int, then via PDZ R-046 to Emmey Int, then via PDZ R-046 to Rustt Int, then via LAX R-068 to Civet Int, then via LAX R-068 to Bindy Int, then via LAX R-068 to Baset Int, then via LAX R-068 to Downe Int. Thence

Twentynine Palms (TNP.DOWNE4): From TNP VOR to Downe Int: Via TNP R-254 to Pione Int, then via LAX R-068 to Rustt Int, then via LAX R-068 to Civet Int, then via LAX R-068 to Bindy Int, then via LAX R-068 to Baset Int, then via LAX R-068 to Downe Int. Thence

ARRIVAL

From Downe Int via SMO R-085 to SMO VOR, then via SMO R-259 to Waker Int. Expect vector to final approach course for Rwys 6 and 7.

Visual Approaches

Usually, if the weather is good and the Pilots have the airport in sight, the Pilots can request a visual approach. Normally this is requested approximately 20 miles outside the airport. What this can do for you, the passenger, is save a minute or two, rather than flying the full instrument approach which takes a little longer.

Before a Pilot is allowed to conduct a visual approach, the Air Traffic Controllers must clear them to do so, and this can only occur if the air traffic flow is safely spaced apart and the weather conditions are good.

If the Pilots are cleared for a visual approach, they will use the same safe descent path as on an instrument approach to the runway. What aids the Pilots in a visual approach to the runway is a series of bar lights known as Visual Approach Slope Indicators, also known as VASI.

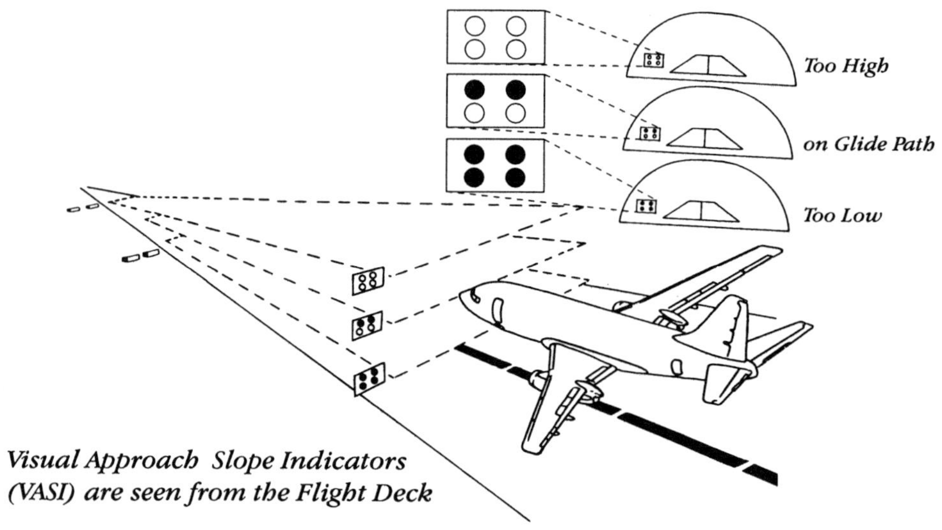

Visual Approach Slope Indicators
(VASI) are seen from the Flight Deck

The VASI provides visual descent guidance by projecting color beams. If you'll notice on the diagram, the colors correspond with the descent angle to the runway. When the glide path is normal, the Pilots will see a red beam projected from the most distant bars, with a white light beam on the bars closest to the end of the runway. Red over white, you're all right!

The VASI system would project a white beam in all of the bars if the glide path were to be too high (shown as two rows of white dots), and red (the two rows of black dots) in all of the bars if the aircraft were to be too low.

The Pilots adjust the angle and speed to remain on the correct glide path until touching down. Now you know why the engine sound changes slightly on the final descent the last minute or two before landing. Considering your aircraft is descending at an approximate speed of 150 miles per hour to come to a safe, smooth, and complete stop in a matter of seconds, it's called "finessing."

Most of the VASI's are located on the left side of the runways. Chances are when you drive near a runway, you see them on the runway as bright red light bars. That's about the only way that you'll see all-red in the bars, because if the Pilot were seeing the all red bars you're seeing in a car, well—let's just say that's not happening!

So you see how very safe the visual approaches can be.

Instrument Landing System—The Final Picture

As you've become familiar with the Departure Procedures and Arrival Procedures, now it's time for the grand finale—the Landing Procedure.

Several types of Landing Procedures are available. It depends on how large and how sophisticated the airport is. The most common type the airlines use is known as the Instrument Landing System, also known as the ILS.

The ILS is very similar to the Departure and Arrival Procedures in that they all use distance from/to the airport, altitude restrictions, and turns.

The first ILS I'd like to explain is the one for a city famous for good barbecue, Kansas City, Missouri ILS.

This ILS will be easy for you if you first find the words "SPICY BARBQ RIBBS MM." You should see them in two places. One set will be located in the top half of the page, also known as the Overview of the Airport, and also in the lower section of the page, known as the Profile.

Beneath the words "SPICY BARBQ RIBBS MM", you'll see the distance from the runway, represented by the D, and in the Profile or side view, you'll also see altitude restrictions. For instance:

SPICY	Means at that point you're 19.7 miles
D19.7	from the runway and should be no
5000'	lower than 5,000 feet

Continuing down the glide path, you'll see BARBQ, which is 13.7 miles out, and you should be no lower than 4,000 feet. Next is RIBBS, 6.7 miles out and your altitude should be no lower than 2,800 feet.

At this point, the aircraft is continuing on instruments or visually (if it's a nice day) for landing. If it's not such a nice day because of fog, thunderstorms, snowstorms, etc., the aircraft will continue down to the minimum altitude. At this time you'll experience either a landing or a go-around, also known as a missed approach. Should this occur, the pilots will either hold, divert, or try again.

Now that you've familiarized yourself with the Instrument Landing System, you're ready to compare your knowledge with two other ILS's, Phoenix, Arizona (ILS to Runway 26R), and Las Vegas, Nevada (ILS to Runway 25L). It's easy.

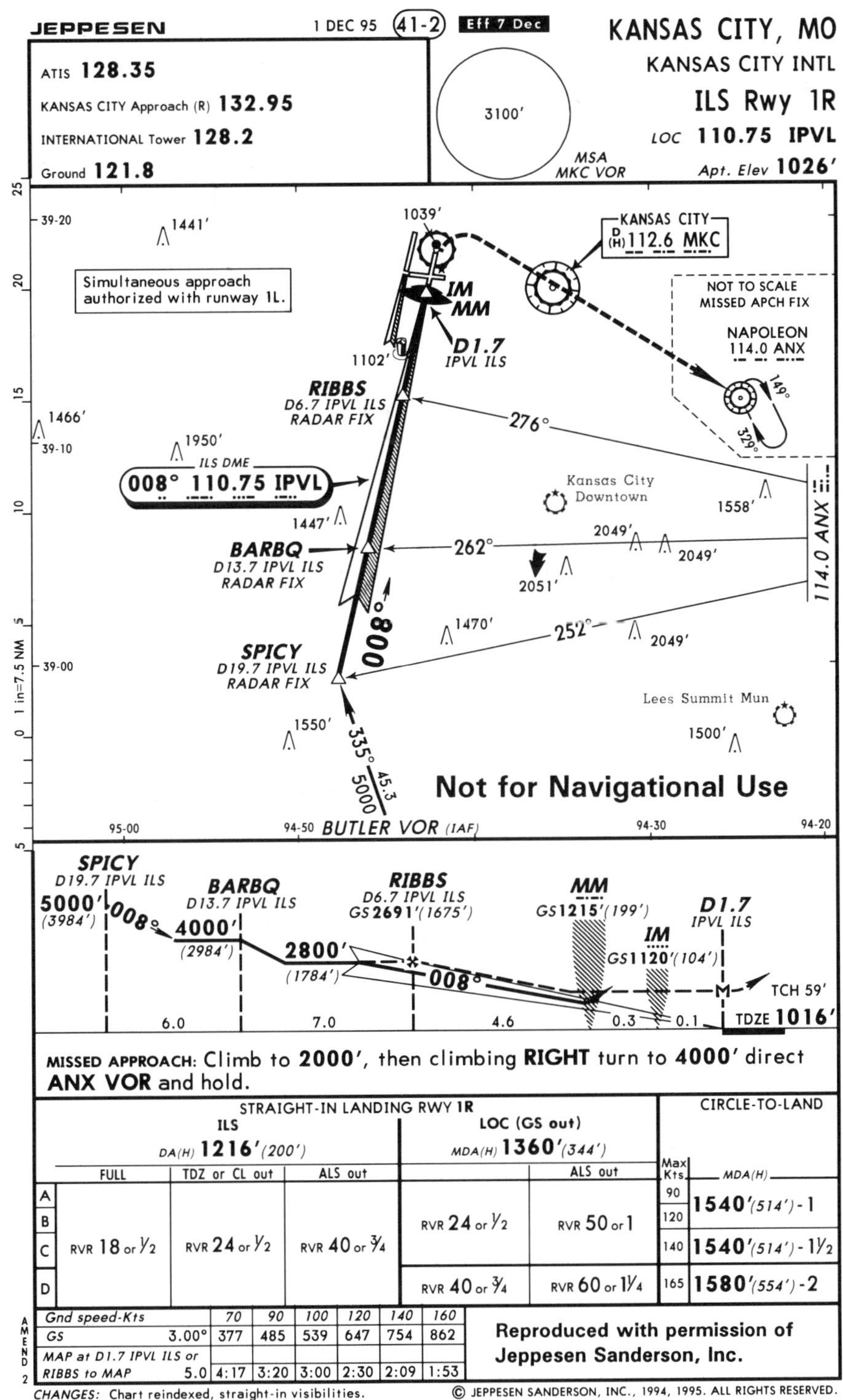

	STRAIGHT-IN LANDING RWY 1R			LOC (GS out)		CIRCLE-TO-LAND	
	ILS DA(H) 1216'(200')			MDA(H) 1360'(344')			
	FULL	TDZ or CL out	ALS out		ALS out	Max Kts	MDA(H)
A						90	1540'(514')-1
B				RVR 24 or ½	RVR 50 or 1	120	
C	RVR 18 or ½	RVR 24 or ½	RVR 40 or ¾			140	1540'(514')-1½
D				RVR 40 or ¾	RVR 60 or 1¼	165	1580'(554')-2

Gnd speed-Kts		70	90	100	120	140	160
GS	3.00°	377	485	539	647	754	862
MAP at D1.7 IPVL ILS or RIBBS to MAP	5.0	4:17	3:20	3:00	2:30	2:09	1:53

AMEND 2

Reproduced with permission of
Jeppesen Sanderson, Inc.

CHANGES: Chart reindexed, straight-in visibilities.

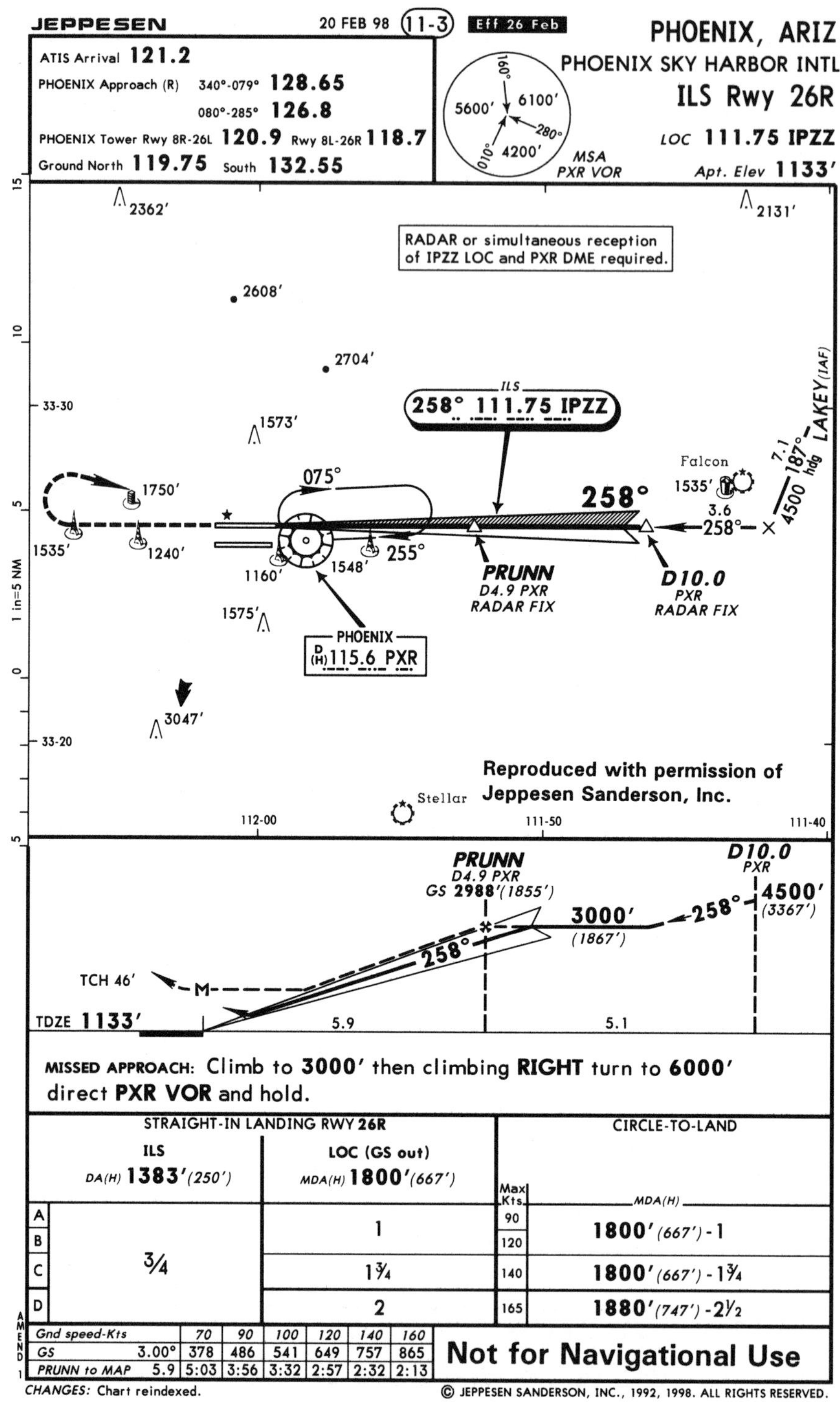

MISSED APPROACH: Climb to **3000'** then climbing **RIGHT** turn to **6000'** direct **PXR VOR** and hold.

STRAIGHT-IN LANDING RWY 26R				CIRCLE-TO-LAND	
ILS DA(H) 1383' (250')	LOC (GS out) MDA(H) 1800' (667')		Max Kts	MDA(H)	
A		1	90	1800' (667') -1	
B			120		
C	3/4	1¾	140	1800' (667') -1¾	
D		2	165	1880' (747') -2½	

Gnd speed-Kts		70	90	100	120	140	160
GS	3.00°	378	486	541	649	757	865
PRUNN to MAP	5.9	5:03	3:56	3:32	2:57	2:32	2:13

Not for Navigational Use

CHANGES: Chart reindexed.

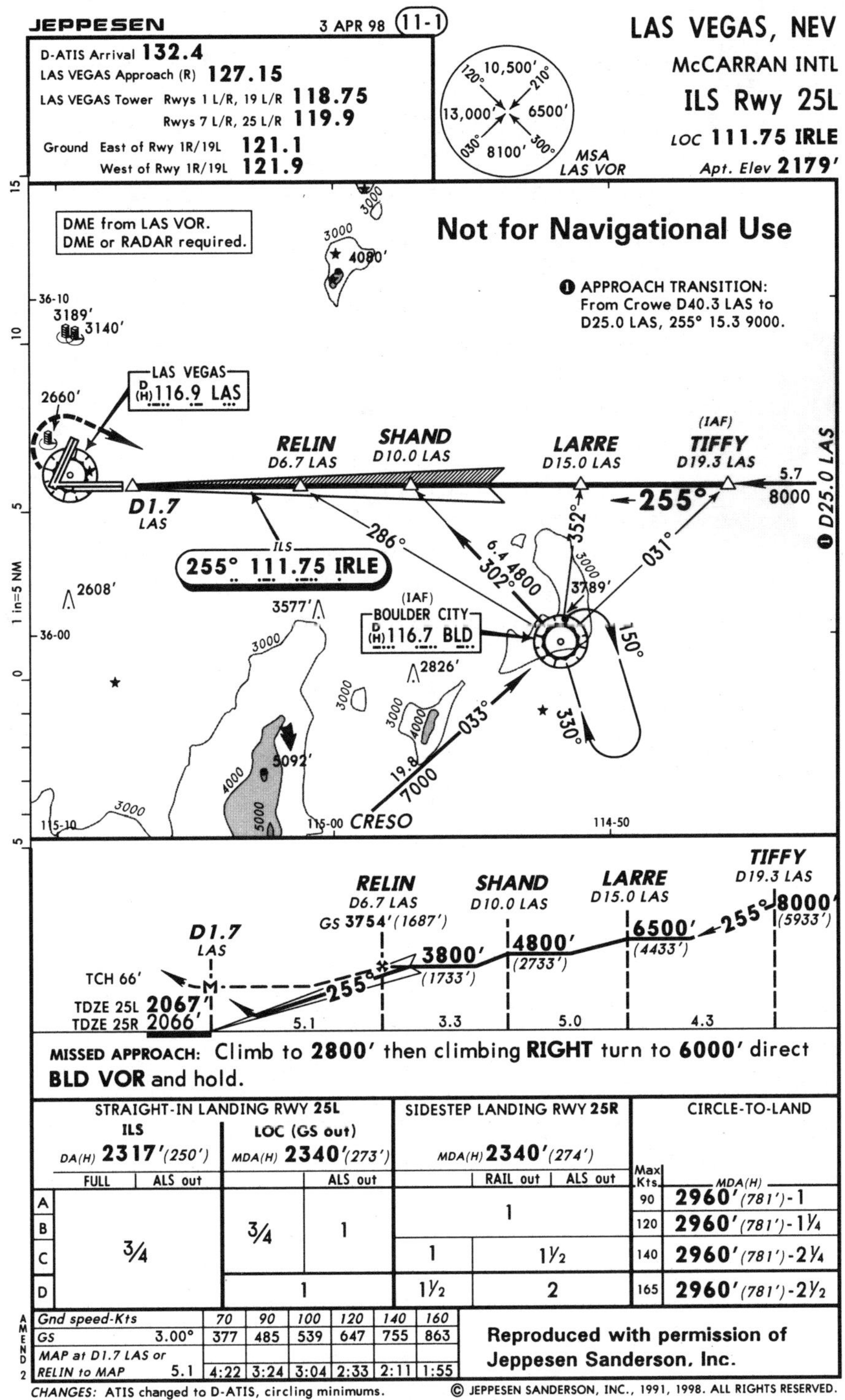

| | STRAIGHT-IN LANDING RWY 25L | | | SIDESTEP LANDING RWY 25R | | Max Kts. | CIRCLE-TO-LAND |
| | ILS | LOC (GS out) | | | | | |
	FULL	ALS out	ALS out	RAIL out	ALS out		MDA(H)
A				1		90	2960'(781')-1
B	3/4	3/4	1			120	2960'(781')-1¼
C				1	1½	140	2960'(781')-2¼
D			1	1½	2	165	2960'(781')-2½

Gnd speed-Kts		70	90	100	120	140	160
GS	3.00°	377	485	539	647	755	863
MAP at D1.7 LAS or RELIN to MAP	5.1	4:22	3:24	3:04	2:33	2:11	1:55

Reproduced with permission of
Jeppesen Sanderson, Inc.

CHANGES: ATIS changed to D-ATIS, circling minimums.

Speed Brakes

During the descent the Air Traffic Controllers may request the Pilots to slow down and get down to a designated altitude within minutes while maintaining a specific speed. Because jets have a smooth and sleek design, this can be a difficult task. The one thing aircraft designers did install for this purpose are speed brakes.

These brakes are actually panels located on the top section of the wings. When the Pilot uses them in the air, you'll notice these normally flush panels rise up. What this does is increase the drag, allowing the aircraft to increase it's angle of descent without increasing speed. While the speed brake is in use, you'll feel a slight vibration and hear a different noise level.

Just think of it this way . . . when you're driving your car downhill and you extend your arm out the window, you of course feel the drag caused by the extension, and you'll also hear a difference. Well, this is what is going on when the Pilots use the speed brakes. These same panels are used on the ground to aid in slowing the aircraft down, and are then referred to as ground spoilers.

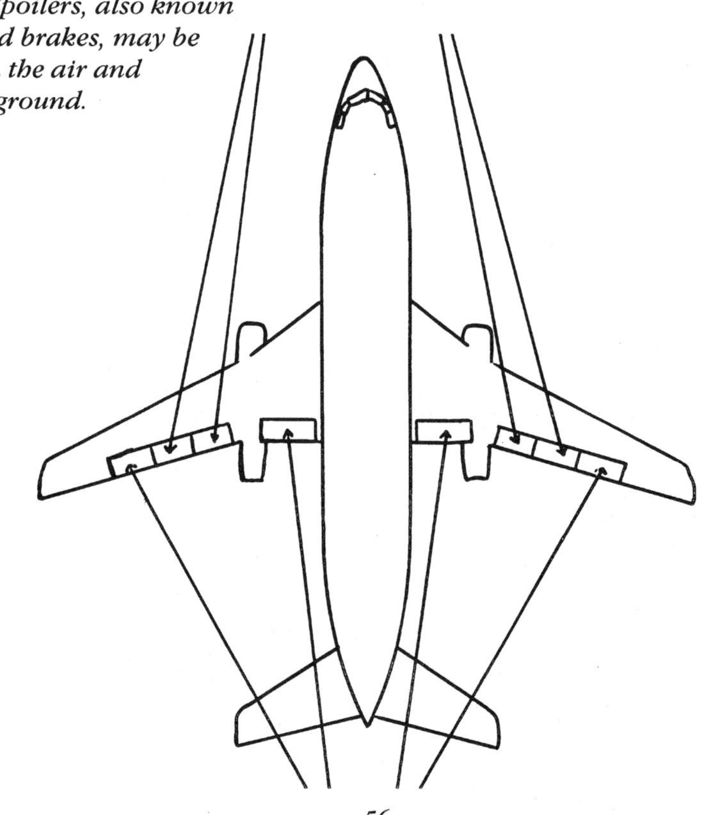

Flight Spoilers, also known as speed brakes, may be used in the air and on the ground.

CHAPTER 12. LANDING

Why are all the landings so different? There are several factors that can affect the smoothness of your landing. Let's consider a few:

1. Weather related landings. Gusty winds, crosswinds, thunderstorms in the area, etc. There are times when the wind is blowing at an angle across the runway. When this happens it is necessary for the Pilot to have one wing lower, or to tilt the airplane, so it will keep on course to the runway.

2. The arriving and departing aircraft's wake.

3. The length of the runway. If a runway is long, the Pilots have more time and distance to work with the local weather conditions. If the runway is short, they must touch down within a specified area, regardless of how smooth it may be, because of the limited distance of remaining runway.

4. Aircraft weight. Lighter aircraft require more work to land smoothly because they have a tendency to float. If the aircraft weight is light when touching down, the struts (landing gear mechanisms) don't compress as much, and this gives a more firm landing.

5. Auto Land. If the aircraft is equipped with the automatic landing capability, the computer can't replace the last few seconds of refinement, as a human can. However, the Auto Land system is an excellent system.

Also, after you've touched down, the braking strength may vary for the above reasons and the Tower Controller may need your aircraft to exit the runway as soon and as safely as possible due to landing traffic or the amount of departures.

Just think—before you judge the landing—the Pilots safely brought you from take-off to landing across cities, mountains, and around weather. So don't judge that entire flight on the last couple of inches.

Airport Information Centers

Did you know that all major airports offer notary services, as well as foreign money exchange, local city maps, travel brochures, informational brochures, postage stamps, envelopes, local and long distance fax service, photocopying, and even phone cards? All these services are available through the Information Center, or in some airports, in the Business Centers. All you have to do is ask at the Information counter and they will assist you or give you directions to meet your needs .

Airport Information Centers' staff are airport representatives, and are not employed by any airline. The airlines have their own airline representatives and are responsible for responding to questions about lost luggage, ticket prices, refunds, seating assignments, etc. In other words, specific airline problems are dealt with by the specific airline, not the Information Center. I'm sure the Information Center representatives would love to help you with specific airline problems, but are not equipped, nor do they have the time, to do so.

The White Courtesy Phone is used to contact the Information Desk representative, who in turn can page another person or give you the message another person has left for you. It does not connect you directly to the other party.

If you have paged someone in the airport and they haven't responded, you can have them paged again. However, it is very important you tell the Information Center representative that it is a second, or updated, page. What this does is reduce the duplicate messages in the computer, allowing the representative to locate your original page.

Because the computer can only show one screen at a time, it reduces the time-consuming effort of locating your previous page.

It's very important to listen to the paging announcements—it could be for you. Although you're not expecting one, someone from the office or home may have an emergency or important message. The pages, as mentioned before, can be unlimited; however, you have to be listening for them in order for them to work.

Lost and Found

All airports have two types of Lost and Found. One is the airport Lost and Found, and the second is for each specific airline. If you should leave an item behind at the gate's boarding area, check with the gate agent first, then the airline's Lost and Found, and last, the airport's Lost and Found.

Luggage

One thing to be aware of is that on the last flight of the day, if you are delayed greatly in getting to the baggage claim, your luggage will be mistaken as unclaimed, and can be locked up until the next day.

It would be wise not to stop at the airport restaurant prior to claiming your luggage. The airlines lock up the unclaimed luggage for your safety.

International Arrival Passengers

International arrival passengers should be met at the International Arrival areas, not at the International Arrival gate. If you go to the gate, you may see your party only briefly before they disappear to Customs. After completing the Customs check, your party will exit in the International Arrival areas, not back at the gate where they disembarked the airplane.

Decreasing Fear of Flying

For those passengers who are most uncomfortable with flying, I recommend the best medicine for you is an introduction to flight, also known as a flight lesson. This also is great for the passenger who would like more knowledge about flying, but doesn't want to become a Pilot.

These are available at all airports that have flight training schools, aircraft rentals, or sightseeing tours. To locate these facilities, just look in the local yellow pages under Aviation, Aircraft Rentals, or Flight Training Schools.

In one flight-hour you'll understand the basic why's and how's to help ease your tension on the larger aircraft. You may love it so much, that you'll sign up for the complete Pilot package—who knows?

Next-Flight Mail, Packages or Cargo

Airlines offer several ways of transporting items such as documents, packages, or cargo that you may need delivered to another destination within hours or perhaps that same day, or 2-day service.

The price, counter-to-counter, is usually:

1-50 pounds, $70.00;

51-70 pounds, $87.00; and

71-100 pounds, $110.00.

All of the above prices vary with each airline and the type of service you choose, as well as the dimensions and destination city. Keep in mind that whether your item weights 1 pound or 50 pounds, it will cost you the minimum amount for that airline.

Should you decide to use this service on a weekend, make sure both departure and arrival cities' cargo facilities are open on the weekend for the type of service you selected.

Pilots

For those who may think that all the Pilots do is sit back and make big bucks, consider how fragile their Pilots license is, and how much knowledge they need to have in a second's time.

Pilots must complete flight simulator training every 6 months and respond to, without error, a multitude of aircraft malfunctions and make a safe landing, regardless of the malfunctions. Some of these malfunctions include: engine fires, engine failures, loss of pressurization, complete hydraulic failures, loss of electrical power, rejected take-offs, minimum visibility landings, and go-arounds (when the aircraft almost lands, and then begins climbing because of weather, traffic, or Air Traffic Controllers' request). All of the above can be given in combination in the simulator, which is nicknamed the "stimulator". With all of the above training, should anything on your flight go "out of the normal" from take-off to landing, the Pilots will be ready for it without any problems.

If the Pilots do not perform to company and FAA standards the airline will usually terminate their employment. In addition, the FAA can revoke all Pilot's licenses and the Pilots cannot re-qualify for at least 1 year. There is no "gray area" in the airlines when it comes to safety, it's black and white.

In addition to the simulator, the Pilots attend ground school, usually once a year. The ground school includes review of aircraft systems, procedures, policies, aircraft limitations, and lectures. There are examinations on all these subjects.

Besides the simulator and ground school, the Pilots are subjected to FAA representatives riding in the flight deck, performing route checks. During the route checks, the FAA checks Pilots' knowledge about aircraft systems, airspace limitations and rules, and weather as well as ensuring that all company procedures are being followed.

Another fragile certificate is the medical certification. Airline Captains must have an extensive physical every 6 months. The First Officers must have one every year. The Second Officers (Flight Engineers) must have one every 24 months. Depending on age, Pilots must have an EKG with the medical examination. If Pilots fall short on their medical exam in any area, their medical certification can be suspended until they meet the minimum requirements. In this case, they are also suspended from flight duty as well.

Unlike many professions (where, when making a lateral move, people may retain their title, position, and pay), the airlines are generally different. When changing airlines, generally the Pilot loses all seniority, titles, and receives a pay decrease. For instance: a Captain with 10 years experience, making X dollars, would become the most junior Co-Pilot or Flight Engineer, with first-year airline pay. The long-range advantage can be an eventual increase in pay, medical benefits, and retirement benefits. When you see your First Officer (Co-Pilot), and are wondering whether or not they are allowed to land the aircraft, not only do they fly, they might have been a 10-year Captain before joining the airline you are flying on.

On this note, did you know the Captain and First Officer alternate flying duties? For instance: the Captain will fly from City A to City B, and the First Officer will fly from City C to City D. Whoever is not actively flying the aircraft will normally make all the radio calls to the Air Traffic Controllers and give all the announcements to the passengers, although the Captain always has the final authority on the entire aircraft and all situations.

Flight Attendants

Through the years, I've heard passengers' remarks about Flight Attendants. If you only see the Flight Attendant making announcements or assisting in the in-flight services, the flight is going smoothly. If you were to see what they're really trained to do, I'd say that you are, at that point, NOT on a boring flight!

Flight Attendants are trained to:

1. Perform CPR;

2. Administer general first aid;

3. Assist when a stroke, heart attack, panic attack, or diabetic seizure occurs;

4. Assist in child birth;

5. Evacuate an aircraft on land or water within minutes; and

6. Determine if a passenger is too incapacitated to fly (i.e., has medical or alcohol-related problems), and if they need assistance in being removed from the flight for the safety of themselves, as well as the other passengers.

Those are just a few of the areas in which they are trained. Please keep this in mind as they assist you during your flight.

Alcohol Aloft

The airlines have encountered a few passengers who wonder why they are limited on alcohol intake. In other words, why can't they get drunk when they're not driving?

The reason for the limitation is that if there is an emergency evacuation, the intoxicated passenger may not be able to help themselves in the evacuation, and also may hinder other passengers in the process.

It has been proven that after a certain amount of alcohol consumption, one's attitude can change to a "No fear. I'm in charge." attitude, which can lead to obvious problems with other passengers as well as crew members.

Another reason why the airlines can't allow you to become intoxicated is that "intoxicated behavior" can lead to a Federal offense if it interferes with the operation of the aircraft.

The Federal Aviation Regulation 91.11, Prohibition Against Interference With Crewmembers, states: "No person may assault, threaten, intimidate, or interfere with a crewmember in the performance of the crewmember's duties aboard an aircraft being operated."

Should this violation occur, the Captain has the authority to divert the aircraft and land at the nearest airport. It only takes a matter of minutes from an altitude of 37,000 feet to land and to have the passenger met by Federal authorities, who in turn can have the passenger in jail before they have time to get a hangover!

The airlines will not tolerate this behavior because it affects the safety of the intoxicated passenger, other passengers, Flight Crew members, as well as the aircraft. So please . . . "Don't even go there."

Did you know that the effects of alcohol increase with altitude, whether you are in a high-elevation city or in the aircraft?

The aircraft is normally pressurized to approximately 5,500 feet for your safety and comfort as it flies at the higher altitude. This air pressure is similar to that at Denver, Colorado. For each drink you have the alcohol effects increase approximately to one or two drinks more than you've consumed. (Just a fact I thought you might like to know.) And no, the airlines don't charge extra for this!

Please be careful with your consumption . . . when, where, and how much.

Flight Recorder and Voice Recorder

Did you ever wonder what the "black boxes", also known as the Flight and Voice Recorders, record? Well, first of all they're not black—they're orange! The recorders themselves may be black, but they're stored in a bright orange container. This makes them easier to locate after an accident.

The Flight Recorder has a continuous tape that records the aircraft speed, heading, altitude, vertical acceleration, elapsed time, trip number and day of the month. It also records anytime the microphone is keyed, whether by the Captain, First Officer, or Forward Observer. With that information, it is easy to tell if the aircraft was climbing, descending and/or turning prior to an accident.

The cockpit Voice Recorder is a 30-minute continuous-loop tape that records cockpit conversations, as well as radio transmissions with the use of a microphone in the overhead of the Flight Deck. Anything older than 30 minutes is automatically erased. This is how the FAA can determine the cause of accidents or incidents.

Scheduled Arrival Times

Although you have a scheduled arrival time, as you can tell after reading this book it can vary.

If you are expecting someone to meet you at your destination, it would be wise to have them call the airline to check on the new arrival time. All airlines try to keep the scheduled arrival time the same as the actual arrival time. Due to headwinds, tailwinds, weather or air traffic congestion, the arrival time can vary.

After departure, the pilots call in the estimated time of arrival (ETA) based on the lift-off or wheels-up time. Prior to descent, the pilots call the arrival city approximately 30 minutes out with the estimated arrival time. At this time, the airlines will update the schedule to reflect changes (if any).

I hope the information I've provided helps you enjoy every aspect of your trip.

I would like to thank each and every one of you for choosing to read this book.

I hope that it brings to you more knowledge, great confidence, and a brighter outlook on airlines before, during, and after your flight.

If you would like to contact me, please write to:

Jan C. Ramos

P.O. Box 130

Rocklin, CA 95677

Once again, thank you for sharing your time with me.

INDEX

A

B

C

D

E

F

G

About the Author

Jan C. Ramos is one of those fortunate people who is living her dream.

After years of collecting degrees, earning licenses, serving her country in the military, and flying freighters all over the world, she now works for a major airline.

For a Pilot, flying for a major airline is the pinnacle. It's a job that only the best get—nothing more than a dream for most Pilots.

Ramos' qualifications? A first-rate record, multiple license rating qualifications, and more than 10,000 hours flying all over the world in all types of aircraft.

She holds an A.A. degree in Aviation from Anchorage Community College, and a B.S. degree in Aeronautics from Embry Riddle Aeronautical University.

She first qualified for her private Pilot's license in 1975, and currently holds six additional licenses and two different type ratings (Captain-qualified): Commercial Pilot; Instrument Pilot; Multi-engine Pilot; Turbo Jet Flight Engineer; Airline Transport Pilot; L382/ C-130 type rating; Boeing 737 type rating; and Certified Flight Instructor.

She was the first female Captain of the civilian version of the C-130 Hercules and also Captained the first commercial cargo flight with an all-female Flight Crew.

The four-engine C-130 Hercules (a cargoliner with a 50,000 pound payload and a 3,000 mile range) has often been described as a "whale with wings", and has long been regarded by Pilots as a "macho" aircraft. The sight of five-foot, five-inch, 120-pound Captain Ramos emerging from the Herc's flight deck in contrast to the massive aircraft is a sight which has raised eyebrows on ramps from New Jersey to New Guinea!!

She has flown such exotic missions as foodlifts to Ethiopia, a helicopter to New Guinea, firefighting equipment to battle Canadian forest fires, and numerous flights to Hawaii, Bermuda, Newfoundland, Central and South America. All this in addition to regular, scheduled flights within the United States.

Ramos served as an Aircraft Electrician in the U.S. Air Force, and honed her flying skills in sunny Florida and snowy Alaska (where she spent 6 years of her 8-year tour.)

Her inspiration to write this book stems from her genuine love of flying and her desire to "de-mystify" this remarkable mode of transportation for those "civilians" who fly (or are planning to), so they will have a better understanding and appreciation of their flying experiences. Hopefully this book will amaze and amuse you—but most importantly—she hopes it will give you knowledge which will enable you to confidently and safely enjoy your excursions into the "wild blue yonder"!